# Pathways of Peace

This book explores the close interconnection that exists between socio-logical and philosophical scholarship in relation to peace studies. Through an examination of the thought of nine leading philosophers and sociolo-gists in their historical and geographical context, the author considers notions of nonviolent resistance, pacifism and reverse strike, as well as violence theories of conflict, theories of conflict resolution, the problem of war, and political transitions towards democratization. Engaging with the work of Thoreau, Gandhi, Ghaffar Khan, Capitini, Dolci, Bobbio, Galtung, Sharp and Weil, and considering the institutionalization of peace research, this volume will appeal to scholars and students of sociology, politics and philosophy with interest in peace and security studies, and conflict.

**Romina Gurashi** is Assistant Professor of Sociology at Sapienza University of Rome, Italy, and the co-author of *Historic and Sociologic Reasons for the Transformation of Abkhazia's Ethnic Conflict* and *From Intractability to Appeasement: A Federal Perspective on the Abkhaz–Georgian Conflict.*

# Pathways of Peace

## The Philosophy and Sociology of Peace and Nonviolence

## Romina Gurashi

Routledge
Taylor & Francis Group

LONDON AND NEW YORK

First published 2019
by Routledge

2 Park Square, Milton Park, Abingdon, Oxfordshire OX14 4RN
52 Vanderbilt Avenue, New York, NY 10017

*Routledge is an imprint of the Taylor & Francis Group, an informa business*

First issued in paperback 2020

Copyright © 2019 Romina Gurashi

The right of Romina Gurashi to be identified as author of this work has
been asserted by her in accordance with sections 77 and 78 of the
Copyright, Designs and Patents Act 1988.

All rights reserved. No part of this book may be reprinted or reproduced or
utiliscd in any form or by any electronic, mechanical, or other means, now
known or hereafter invented, including photocopying and recording, or in
any information storage or retrieval system, without permission in writing
from the publishers.

Notice:
Product or corporate names may be trademarks or registered trademarks,
and are used only for identification and explanation without intent to
infringe.

*British Library Cataloguing-in-Publication Data*
A catalogue record for this book is available from the British Library

*Library of Congress Cataloging-in-Publication Data*
Names: Gurashi, Romina, author.
Title: Pathways of peace : the philosophy and sociology of peace and
nonviolence / Romina Gurashi.
Description: Abingdon, Oxon ; New York, NY : Routledge, 2019. |
Includes bibliographical references and index.
Identifiers: LCCN 2018021583| ISBN 9780815377870 (hbk) |
ISBN 9781351233620 (ebk)
Subjects: LCSH: Nonviolence. | Peace.
Classification: LCC HM1281 .G87 2019 | DDC 303.6/1--dc23
LC record available at https://lccn.loc.gov/2018021583

ISBN: 978-0-8153-7787-0 (hbk)
ISBN: 978-0-367-60681-7 (pbk)

Typeset in Times New Roman
by Taylor & Francis Books

# Contents

# Figures

# Acknowledgments

It is with simple and sincere gratitude that I say "thank you" to my two mentors Roberta Iannone and Maria Cristina Laurenti for instilling in me a passion for research and a determination to pursue my dreams.

Thanks also to Alessandro and Hoze for supporting me in every step, and to my beloved mother Ermelinda and my beloved father Kolë for always being there for me.

# Introduction

Dealing seriously with peace and nonviolence issues is crucial today. In a world suffering from conflicts, where indicators of global peace have decreased by 2.14% since 2008, where safety and security issues have registered a negative trend of 61% in countries suffering from deteriorating conditions of peace, where violence has cost almost $1.04 trillion (USD), or 12.6% of world GDP,[1] defeatist and passive stances cannot be adopted.

There is a need to choose an appropriate understanding of such phenomena if we want to have an impact on them. Knowing the history and paths of development of the concepts of nonviolence and peace, understanding their historical, politico-philosophical and sociological evolution is the only way to discover the instruments needed to change the reality. We too often forget that mankind, together with its aspirations, choices, beliefs, symbols and religiosity, is the only one who can shape reality and fill it with meaning. Reality is the result of actions taken by men and women, on the basis of their knowledge, intuitions and experience. Such choices can have consequences not only for those individuals but also for their groups, their communities and society as a whole. Just as the circular waves emanating from a stone thrown in water become wider and wider while decreasing in their intensity, the aftermaths of the actions and choices we make can spread within society.

In this perspective, understanding how individuals see and live reality is as important as understanding the political mechanisms and power relations of the international community. Therefore, far from being abstractions, peace and war are constructs we create through our actions, conditioned by culture, traditions, beliefs, religions and so on. This means that peace and war are the expression of human action, both individual and collective, and are not abstract phenomena belonging only to the sphere of the intelligible.

This work is aimed at analyzing how ways of considering peace and war both at an individual and at a collective level have changed, by studying social movements and ideas of some of the main contemporary philosophers and sociologists. The objective is to show the close interconnection between research in the fields of sociology and philosophy and peace studies. Although some researchers in peace studies have asserted in general terms how strongly the study of peace is interconnected with philosophy, history, economics and psychology, currently there is no methodical study of the points of contact between philosophical and sociological theories in the field. This extensive study (extensive from the point of the number of authors considered) is intended to fill this gap. Through the analysis of the theories, ideas and actions of nine important historical figures – Henry David Thoreau, Mohandas Karamchand Gandhi, Abdul Ghaffar Khan, Simone Weil, Aldo Capitini, Danilo Dolci, Johan Galtung and Gene Sharp – I will demonstrate the genesis and current developments of the concepts of nonviolence and peace, both in a philosophical and a sociological perspective. The aim therefore is to identify the pathways of nonviolence and peace that periodically interweave but frequently proceed in parallel directions in these authors.

The first chapter will focus on the concepts of civil disobedience and nonviolence in Henry David Thoreau, Mohandas K. Gandhi and Abdul Ghaffar Khan's writings and ideas contextualizing them in terms of abolitionism in the United States and the independence movements in Asia. The second chapter will investigate the European matrices of peace and nonviolence, which will be described through an analysis of the ideas of Simone Weil on the problem of war, Aldo Capitini on religious nonviolence, Danilo Dolci on the reverse strike and Norberto Bobbio on institutional pacifism. Subsequently – in the third chapter – we will focus on the heterogeneous development of the approaches to research in this field and on the origins of the first academic institutions oriented to the study of peace. The fourth and the fifth chapters will then be devoted to a brief analysis of the two leading contemporary authors on peace and nonviolence: Johan Galtung, a European sociologist concerned with the study of peace, violence and conflict transformation; and Gene Sharp, an American philosopher whose main activity was in the field of nonviolence and civil resistance.

## Note

1   Data provided by the *Global Peace Index 2017* (IEP 2017).

## References

IEP (Institute for Economics and Peace) (2017) *Global Peace Index 2017: Measuring Peace in a Complex World*, Rep. 48, Vision of Humanity [portal], IEP, <http://visionofhumanity.org/app/uploads/2017/06/GPI17-Report.pdf> (accessed 19 October 2017).

# 1 On civil disobedience and nonviolence

## The socio-ethical origins of civil disobedience

The origins of civil disobedience can be traced back to the United States in the early nineteenth century. It was a period of radical changes, contrasts and socio-ethical dilemmas. The War of Independence from British rule had just ended, the US Constitution had come into force, giving rise to a national debate over the protection of the slave trade, and expansionist appetites were looking westward to snatch up new territories. This led to a spate of wars against Native Americans and the promulgation, in 1830, of the Indian Removal Act, the annexation of French Louisiana, the war against Britain in 1812 to settle trade disputes, the annexation of Florida, and later, in 1845, the annexation of Texas.

Thus, conflict became a daily reality to be reckoned with, provoking political and religious figures to confront the political, economic and social issues that from time to time emerged from needs related to the state of war.

Discontent over this state of affairs, socio-ethical dilemmas and religious principles led to the publication of "what we might consider the first manifesto of the nonviolent movement" (Losurdo 2010: 9): David Low Dodge's *War Inconsistent with the Religion of Jesus Christ*. This ethico-religious treatise listed the reasons why war was irreconcilable with Christian teachings. The work preached an absolute vision of pacifism, condemning all manner of violence – even recourse to self-defence – in relations between persons as in those between nations. In his essay, Dodge claimed that even carrying a weapon made for an attitude contrary to the teachings of Christ. Violence was to be considered an inhuman act to be avoided even if it meant challenging the authority of governments and rulers who had acted in violation of the word of God. Consequently, he claimed that the spirit of martyrdom was the spirit of Christianity and that any action aimed at legitimizing violence and opposing the Sermon on the Mount should be considered criminal.

In August 1815, following the publication of his essay, Dodge created the New York Peace Society, the first of its kind in the US and, for that matter, in the world at large. The Society involved itself in spreading anti-militarist literature and in other ways proselytizing by narrating the horrors of war and campaigning for a radical vision of peace as preached in the gospels. In 1828, the society merged with its homologues in New Hampshire, Maine and Massachusetts to form the American Peace Society. This larger body organized peace conferences and published the periodical *Advocate of Peace*. In 1838, from the American Peace Society an offshoot was born, the American New England Non-Resistance Society, which, like those that had preceded it, promoted a return to a primitive Christianity but also added the philosophy of "non-resistance" and the inclusion of women in its public political activities. This group's proselytizing message was considered especially radical by its more moderate members, as it not only rejected all manner of violence but also denied any distinction based on race, nationality or gender difference (Walters 1997: 120). The novelty of this association lay in its will to distance itself from Old Testament truculence, the legitimization of holy wars, and violence in all its forms, for "God did not limit to individuals the precepts of the Gospels, which were also valid for nations" (Losurdo 2010: 10). Another novelty, even for the Quakers, who had hitherto rejected violence between nations and called for European peace, was its outcry for the abolition of slavery.

These movements could only have been inspired by the French Revolution, child of the Enlightenment that wished to abolish slavery and encourage – with the downfall of the *Ancien Régime* – the hope of a future of peace free from the scourge of war. The Enlightenment as a political, social and cultural movement had pervaded every aspect of contemporary human life and celebrated Reason as an instrument for improving one's personal condition.

Many ideas and events related to the Enlightenment, such as the French Revolution and the Industrial Revolution, inevitably influenced the traditional behavior and attitudes of many countries (Cebi 2011: 306):

> The intellectual leadership of the Enlightenment came from prominent men of letters (as they called themselves) such as the French philosophers Voltaire, Denis Diderot, and Jean le Rond d'Alembert; the Swiss writer Jean-Jacques Rousseau; the Scottish philosophers Adam Smith and David Hume; the German philosophers Moses Mendelssohn, Immanuel Kant, and Gotthold Ephraim Lessing; the US politician and philosopher Thomas Jefferson; and the Italian politician and philosopher Beccaria (Cesare, Marquis de Beccaria-Bonsan); to name just a few.
>
> (Garrard 2011: 508)

These eminent figures, united by a common vision of the world and common beliefs in the fields of science, politics, morality and religion, although they did not share a common project, were nonetheless signposts for the philosophers and sociologists who later grappled with the problems of citizens' rights, the limits of the state, science, ethics and religion.

With regard to the quest for peace and the rights of citizens it is especially important to recall the contributions of certain Enlightenment intellectuals.

First of all, Locke and Voltaire, who promoted a more radical, expanded version of the principles of tolerance already present in the Greco-Roman world. In his *Letter on Tolerance* (1685) Locke presented his ideas on this subject by condemning any Church that attempted to coercively impose its brand of worship, calling them "false Churches" as opposed to the "true Churches" that based their actions on principles of mutual respect. Locke opposed the historical tendency of religion to foment pretexts for wars or justify massacres. Religion was meant to be a precept aimed at nurturing virtue and pity in the souls of human beings rather than an instrument of violence.

In his *Treatise on Tolerance* (1763), Voltaire too dealt with the problem of religious fanaticism and the consequent problem of intolerance. Shocked by the trial and execution of Jean Calas, Voltaire used the major cases of judicial error (those of Calas, Sirven and La Barre) to defend the right to reason freely and to criticize the authoritarianism and traditionalism that were typical of the French absolutism of that period. The key issues of his treatise were the peaceful coexistence of citizens within the state and the need to enforce the fundamental human rights:

> We dare to believe, in honor of the century in which we live, that there is not one enlightened man in Europe who does not consider tolerance as a right of justice, a duty prescribed by humanity, conscience, religion; a law necessary for the peace and prosperity of states. [...] Freedom of opinion, that of professing it publicly and conforming to it in one's conduct for all that does not violate the rights of another man, is just as real a right as that of personal freedom or private property. Thus, any limitation affecting the exercise of this right is contrary to justice, and any intolerant law is an unjust law. [...] The general interest of humanity, this first objective of all virtuous hearts, requires freedom of opinion, conscience and worship: firstly, because this is the only way to establish true brotherhood among men; for since it is impossible to unite them in the same religious opinions, it is necessary to teach them to consider, to treat as their own brothers those who have opinions contrary to theirs. [...] Could politics have any other convictions?
>
> (Voltaire 2006: 25)

What is clear from this excerpt is that Voltaire's tolerance was not a simple acknowledgment of the limits of human nature; it was not forbearance, indulgence or indifference. Tolerance originated in an analysis of human nature and was the fertile ground on which to mount a political movement for equality of rights and freedom of opinion, worship and conscience.

This line of reasoning also includes Cesare Beccaria's *Dei delitti e delle pene* (On crimes and punishments) written in 1764. In this brief essay, the Italian jurist tried to "humanize" the concept of punishment by demonstrating the paradoxes related to such practices as torture, corporeal punishment and the death penalty:

> Abolishing practices that caused bodily pain was also a means to a larger political end, namely, creating legal institutions and practices that would act on the soul and mind, not the body. Beccaria's vision sought to institute new "enlightened" practices that would cultivate habits of disciplined labour and nonviolent future-oriented thought amongst the offenders; and at the same time cultivate humane civilized sensibilities among the public.
>
> (Valverde 2017: 44)

The need to punish was therefore justified and justifiable only if it guaranteed social order and safety. This scrutiny of punishment, of its proportionality to the crime and its limits, became an indispensable element in the movement to promote individual freedoms and the most important human aspiration: love.

Immanuel Kant was another great Enlightenment figure who, in his essay *Perpetual Peace: A Philosophical Sketch* (1795), reflected on freedom as a theorization of the best form of the state and the reforms needed to build world peace. He wrote the work in reaction to the Peace of Basel, agreed on between Revolutionary France and Prussia, which he regarded as a merely temporary truce.

His text was structured according to a normative form made up of six "preliminary" articles, three "definitive" articles, two supplements and a two-part appendix on morals and politics. The linchpin of the essay lay precisely in these three definitive articles. The first regarded the "republican" state as the *conditio sine qua non* for peace, where "republican" did not mean opposition to monarchy, but opposition to despotism. This form of state, founded on freedom, equality and dependence on a single common body of law, would be better than others because the sovereign, now a citizen of the state, would, in the event of war, not be "the owner of the state – who – […] does not lose a whit by the war, while he goes on enjoying the delights of his table or sport, or of his pleasure palaces and gala days" (Kant 1903: 123).

In order for perpetual peace to come about, it was also necessary for republics to join a confederation, "which we may call a covenant of peace (*foedus pacificum*), which would differ from a treaty of peace (*pactum pacis*) in this respect, that the latter merely puts an end to one war, while the former would seek to put an end to war forever" (Kant 1903: 134). This condition would be more easily achieved if the relationship between states and foreigners were followed by the logic of *universal hospitality* in an attempt to pursue a cosmopolitan constitution.

Projects to overcome violence in favor of perpetual and universal peace through a republican system were discounted by the outbreak of war, between 1812 and 1815, between the two countries with the most advanced republican constitutions, the United States and Great Britain.

This circumstance led to general disillusionment toward the possibility of universal peace. Karl Marx and Friedrich Engels themselves – despite their appreciation of the French Revolution and familiarity with Kant's *Perpetual Peace* – believed that a universal peace could be achieved only by doing away with a socio-political system based on one class oppressing another. In fact, "within the various socialist currents war has always been considered a product not so much of a certain type of political regime as of a certain form of production, to wit the capitalist variety, whose survival depends on the continual conquest of new markets" (Bobbio 2007: 665).

Going back to the America of the mid-1800s, we can see how the relationship between the individual and the state, the rejection of slavery and wars of conquest were at the center of Henry David Thoreau's commitment to individual civil liberty.

## The civil disobedience of Henry David Thoreau

In contrast to the ethos of the pacifist movements of his day, Thoreau's thought was marked by a strong secularism. His essay *Civil Disobedience* was originally written in 1848 as a speech to be given at the Concord Lyceum with the title "Resistance to Civil Government" and was later published as we know it today.

The work was the result of his personal opposition to the war then being waged by the United States against Mexico (1845–48), which Thoreau – opposed to US aggressiveness and slavery – intended to defy by refusing to pay taxes. He was sent to jail for his stand, though he spent only one night there, as an aunt of his, unbeknownst to him, paid the tax on his behalf.

*Civil Disobedience* opened with the idea that the best government was one that governed less, or rather, it affirmed "that government is best which governs not at all" (Thoreau 1866: 123). However, this was a goal that could only be achieved by an adequate social maturity.

For the moment the abolition of government, as the anarchist groups desired, was unthinkable, but what could be demanded in the short term was a better government than the inefficient one under which the citizenry was forced to live:

> After all, the practical reason why, when the power is once in the hands of the people, a majority are permitted, and for a long period continue, to rule, is not because they are most likely to be in the right, nor because it seems fairest to the majority, but because they are physically the strongest.
>
> (Thoreau 1866: 125)

So, a fundamental question remained: "Can there not be a government in which the majorities do not virtually decide right and wrong, but conscience?" (Thoreau 1866: 125). To what extent must a citizen abandon his conscience into the hands of the legislator? These were fundamental questions for modern society and the answer could be considered revolutionary: it was necessary to be human beings before being subjects, and therefore unjust norms should not be respected, in contrast with one's own personal conscience. The only obligation for an individual was therefore reduced to acting according to their own conscience so as not to become an instrument of the majority.

And his personal criticism of pro-slavery governments stemmed precisely from this criticism of people who relinquish their conscience and allow themselves to be brainwashed by the state. Unlike the British philosopher and theologian William Paley, who resolved the issue of submission to civil government as a question of coexistence, believing that this should take place on condition that an established government could be fought or changed without public harm, Thoreau believed that a rebellion of the honest was admissible and not at all premature, since the state in which these citizens lived had been guilty of dreadful crimes such as the enslavement of one-sixth of its population and the invasion of a foreign country (Mexico). "Under a government which imprisons any unjustly, the proper place for a just man is also a prison" because it is the only place "in a slave state in which a free man can abide with honor" (Thoreau 1866: 136–37).

It should be noted, however, that Thoreau, while preferring peaceful civil disobedience, did not rule out the need to use violence, and for this reason gave moral and political support to John Brown, the armed prophet of the Southern slave revolt (Losurdo 2010: 23). Nonetheless, his essay on civil disobedience inspired a far more irenic approach to nonviolence in subsequent years. Thoreau's essay on civil disobedience was indeed a great inspiration to Tolstoy, Gandhi and Martin Luther King, all of whom found in this little essay the inspiration for a new kind of political and moral struggle.

## *Ahimsa* and Truth at the service of *satyagraha* in Gandhi

A relay point of nonviolent thought and civil disobedience from the US to India was the British Empire, which dominated one quarter of habitable lands at that time. Among these there were India and South Africa, where a new kind of indentured slavery had been established for the Chinese or Indian ethnic groups, that of the *coolies*.

It was precisely the problem of the coolies and the discrimination that the Indians were subjected to in South Africa that spurred the activity of the young Mohandas Karamchand Gandhi, who went to South Africa as a legal consultant for an Indian company, Dada Abdullah & Co., and remained there for twenty years, during which time he succeeded through *satyagraha*, a particular method of nonviolent struggle, in abrogating some important discriminatory laws and obtaining the recognition of the equal rights of the citizens residing there.

In 1915, on his return to India, he continued his work of resistance to discrimination and the Empire, even participating in the Indian National Congress (1921). He led campaigns at the national level to fight poverty, demand the recognition of women's rights, try to abolish untouchability and increase India's economic and political autonomy with the final assumption of *swaray*, total independence from foreign domination. It was a very hard path to take and, on many occasions, both in Africa and in India, he underwent summary detention and imprisonment, facing these experiences with a spirit of sacrifice and humility and achieving, in 1947, India's total independence.

Gandhi's philosophico-political thought suffers from a problem of medium, since his writings consisted mainly of newspaper articles (written for the *Indian Opinion*, the *Harijan* and the *Young India*), personal correspondence and appeals almost always written to clarify his position on certain events or initiatives. A lack of systematizing attributable to the non-definitive, experimental character of his ethico-political convictions, as he himself clarified in an issue of *Harijan* of 28 March 1936: "the opinions I have formed and the conclusions I have reached are not definitive. I might change them at any time" (Gandhi 1996: 5).

Furthermore, the lack of an actual treatise on nonviolence is to be attributed to the fact that he was a man of action, not a scholar, and as long as he was alive his ideas could not be systematically formulated. Just the same, we can focus on the themes and features of Gandhi's socio-philosophical thought, which placed ethics at the center of a whole theoretical and technical framework of nonviolent action.

His starting point was self-analysis, a necessary tool for a man striving to discover the Truth, first, in relation to himself, and secondly also in relation to others. Although this *truth* was subjective and therefore partial, since only God could know the Absolute Truth – for this reason Gandhi also said that "Truth is God" (Gandhi 2010: 70–71) – human beings had the moral duty to "live according to the truth as they are able to see it, and doing so by resorting to the purest means, that is, to nonviolence" (Gandhi 2010: 70). And only after finding this partial truth would people be able to live ethically in love and faith.

It was precisely on the concept of love that Gandhi's ethics were greatly influenced by the thought of the Russian writer Leo Tolstoy. In fact, by rejecting the classical dualistic conception that distinguished between individual and group ethics, he maintained that there was only one ethics, the *ethics of love*, "valid both for individuals and groups, which prohibits any form of coercion and compulsion and preaches submission to suffering on one's person whenever this is the only alternative to inflicting it on others" (Pontara 2007: 382). An idea of pure love that did not admit any kind of pressure or force, and prevented Tolstoyism from representing a real alternative to violence as an instrument of politics by expelling Tolstoy and his followers from it.

But Gandhi, while not giving up his political struggle, spoke of "*ahimsa*," a Sanskrit word composed of a privative "*a*" and "*himsa*," which meant "violence," "harm," and which indicated the absence of any desire to harm or kill, hence nonviolence, love. *Ahimsa* meant absolute freedom from ill will, anger and hatred, and an overabundant love for everything (Gandhi 1963: 234–35). This different conception of love meant that nonviolence became the sole form of active struggle that opposed the adversary's strength by moral and mental resistance alone, in the belief that one's patience and suffering could convince the other of the error of their reasoning.

This would be a kind of positive conversion made plausible by belief in two fundamental assumptions: (1) the principle that people were born good and could be converted to what was right at any moment of their lives through acts of sacrifice and charity, and (2) the belief that *ahimsa* means love in the Pauline sense of the term: a sentiment that gave meaning to all the actions that individuals carried out.[1] For example, nonviolent struggle itself could not have existed as such without love and faith in God's illuminating our journey. Here, then, is the difference between the thought of Thoreau and that of Gandhi. While Thoreau, still strongly influenced by the Enlightenment, posited civil resistance in a purely secular context, Gandhi had appropriated the teachings of his most illustrious predecessors (including Thoreau himself) to create a new idea of struggle, no longer limited to mere resistance.

*Ahimsa* was therefore the only means to arrive at Truth, a concept that contained not only the truth of words and thoughts, but also God himself. A universal end that could only be pursued if one were able to love the vilest people as oneself and if one were able to put aside one's selfish interests in the ethical realization of a social good. The twin concepts of *ahimsa* and Truth were so closely interdependent as to be considered two sides of the same coin, or better, of a metal disk on which no figure is impressed and of which neither side could be distinguished from the other (Gandhi 1996: 36).

To the Machiavellian-like question of why good ends could not be reached even by violent means, Gandhi replied that good ends could only be achieved by good means since "means can be compared to a seed, and the end to a tree; between the means and the end there is the same inviolable relationship that exists between the seed and the tree" (Gandhi 1996: 44). For Gandhi, therefore, social and political action was closely connected to the religious plane and above all to the ethical plane of Truth and Love. Any reform, any social change, would have to take this high road to arrive at positive results.

Another important concept for Gandhism was "*satyagraha*," a word formed by "*satya*" which meant truth and "*agraha*" which meant firmness, strength, or better "true force," "force of love" or "firmness in truth." The word was coined in 1906 when, during his South African campaign Gandhi realized that the term "passive resistance" was inadequate to define the Indian struggle for civil rights. So, the *Indian Opinion* announced a contest which was won by Maganlal Gandhi (a follower of Mohandas K. Gandhi) with the term *sadagraha* ("firmness in a good cause"), but to make the term more understandable it was changed to *satyagraha*.

With this concept Mohandas Gandhi wanted to distinguish the type of civil disobedience that the Indians were carrying out in South Africa from the passive resistance carried out by John Clifford during the the the controversy over the Education Act of 1902[2] or by the suffragette movement. The suffragettes were not in themselves opposed to the use of force but were aware of their weakness and numerical inferiority, which would never enable them to prevail over the organized majority. Instead, *satyagrahi* (those who practiced the technique of *satyagraha*) had all the necessary requisites to make a successful use of violence, yet they chose to employ only the nonviolent means that had been in keeping with their morality. While Clifford's and the suffragettes' nonviolence was that of the weak, *satyagrahi* was a nonviolence of the strong, "a force that can be used by both individuals and communities. It can be used both in political affairs and in personal matters. Its universal applicability is a demonstration of its effectiveness and invincibility" (Gandhi 1996: 27–28).

To get back to what we spoke of earlier in relation to his difference from Thoreau, Gandhi had also identified what he believed to be the differences between *satyagraha*, passive resistance, civil disobedience, and non-cooperation.

As already mentioned, *satyagraha* was a type of nonviolent technique of struggle that was subject to the force of *ahimsa* and for this reason excluded the use of violence as a means to an end. Violence was also banned because, despite the fact that *satyagrahi* sought Truth, since absolute truth was unknowable one had no right to punish another for their actions.

*Passive resistance* was the tool usually adopted by nonconformists to express their dissent. As already stated, unlike *satyagraha*, this was an instrument of the weak, who avoided violence solely for contingent reasons and did not exclude its future use if the situation made it advantageous.

*Civil disobedience* was characterized by being the deliberate violation of immoral laws, carried out to stress the injustice perpetrated through the adoption of certain norms. It was a strategy characterized by the acceptance without resistance of any subsequent punishment which the practitioners of civil disobedience were subjected to. For Gandhi this was an indispensable tool of *satyagraha*.

And, lastly, *non-cooperation*. The refusal to cooperate with a corrupt state. Unlike civil disobedience, it was not such a radical instrument of struggle, since, though it produced a rift between the state and the individual, it did not involve a rejection of pre-established norms. Obviously, even non-cooperation was an instrument used in *satyagraha*, which contained any form of nonviolent resistance necessary for affirming Truth.

Yet Gandhi's opposition to violence was not a complete abstention from the use of force but represented a willingness to act in such a way that the actions taken should lead to the greatest possible decrease in the use of violence in the world. And this because he was aware that violence was an indispensable tool in the history of humanity.

This awareness led him to explicitly recognize the cases in which the use of this instrument was not only admissible, but even desirable, as for example in resorting to euthanasia for painful and fatal illness; in stopping someone insane from a killing spree; in choosing between cowardice and violence. Taking up the example of the homicidal lunatic, Gandhi claimed that refusing to act for a just cause out of fear would be cowardly, and therefore not in conformity with nonviolence.

The last two points may seem to contrast with the ethical vision so far maintained. Nonetheless, Gandhi himself made it clear that in analyzing the above cases the concepts of *himsa* and *ahimsa* were taken fully into account. In fact, the basis of the distinction between a just action tending to Truth and a wrong one dictated by personal interest and cowardice was precisely the presence or absence of *hymsa*, or the will to cause suffering or to kill with anger, selfish ends or the mere will to do harm.

In this perspective, the most controversial point of Gandhi's thought was the position he took on the wars in his experience. Despite his profession of faith in *ahimsa*, Gandhi did not hesitate to support the British during the Boer War (1899–1902), the war against the Zulus (1906) and the First World War (1914–18). To those who criticized these choices he provided justifications in news articles and public speeches.

As to the Boer War, he claimed that his participation in the ambulance corps was motivated by the fact that "if I demanded that the rights owed to a British citizen be granted to me, it was my duty as such to participate in the defense of the Empire. I thought then that India could completely emancipate itself only with the help of the British Empire" (Gandhi 2010: 167). As to the war against the Zulus, Gandhi chose to take part because he was convinced that the British Empire was really working for the common good. "A sincere sense of loyalty prevented me from ill will toward the Empire. The correctness or not of the 'rebellion' therefore could not influence my decision" (Gandhi 1996: 78). By contrast, his motivation to participate in the First World War as a recruiter was to be found in his desire to cancel any difference in treatment between English and Indians:

> I thought that Indians residing in England should do their duty in war; English students had volunteered in the army, and the Indians should not be outdone. There were many objections and it was observed that there was a great difference between the Indians and the English, we were slaves and they master. Should a slave work with his master when he is in need?
>
> (Gandhi 2010: 259)

Near the end of the First World War, in a letter dated 6 July 1918, in keeping with what had been his position up to that time, he also came to affirm that "in exceptional circumstances war can be a necessary evil, as is the body" (Losurdo 2010: 3).

According to Giuliano Pontara's interpretation of Gandhi's choices, Gandhi condemned the need for violence as a way to resolve conflicts between groups, in the belief that better results could be obtained from nonviolent methods, but

> when Gandhi regards violence as a "lesser evil" he is using this expression in quite a different sense from that in which it is normally used. He intends to say that there are situations in which it is morally better for the actor to choose violence, as for instance in those situations in which the only choice is between violence and cowardice or other morally bad motives for refraining from it.
>
> (Pontara 1965: 200)

Indeed, as previously noted regarding the means–end relationship, Gandhi did not reject violence as an evil in and of itself, but as an instrument unsuited to lead to the moral results he aspired to.

As also highlighted by David Cortright in his masterful work *Peace: A History of Movements and Ideas* (2008), Gandhi mainly aimed at developing the concept of nonviolence and distinguishing it from that of civil resistance. Moreover, as emerges from our discussion so far, Gandhi intended to strip the concept of nonviolence of all those negative elements that characterized it as a denial of violence:

> Ghandhi's meaning was deftly summarized by Jonathan Schell: "Violence is a method by which the ruthless few can subdue the ruthless many. Nonviolence is a means by which the active many can overcome the ruthless few." Yet the word nonviolence is "highly imperfect," wrote Schell. It is a word of "negative construction," as if the most important thing that can be said about nonviolence is that it is *not* something else. It is a negation of the negative force of violence, a double negative which in mathematics would yield a positive result. Yet English has no positive word for it.
>
> (Cortright 2008: 7)

Gandhi had hit upon the real problem. Not only was it necessary to give – at that precise moment in history and for reasons linked to the legitimization of peoples' demands for self-determination – a positive definition of nonviolence to enable it to be an instrument of struggle legally accepted by the regulatory framework, but also to endow the concept with social, economic and political meanings that would give it a full-blown identity and no longer as simply a negation of violence (however direct).

## The nonviolent Islam of Abdul Ghaffar Khan

A long-neglected though very important exponent of a nonviolent, reformist, pacifist current within Islam is Khan Abdul Ghaffar Khan, known in his homeland as the "King of Chiefs" (*Badshah Khan*) or the "Frontier" Gandhi (*Sarhaddi Gandhi*). He was a Pakhtun political and spiritual leader remembered for his nonviolent methods and profound interpretation of Islam and the Koran. His political and social action unfolded during the period of British occupation of the territories of northern Pakistan in the same period in which Gandhi was challenging British rule in India. Although little known in the West, he takes on special importance as a demonstration that there is an Islam that preaches peace, love and

tolerance, and as another tile of the mosaic of nonviolent, pacifist movements that developed between the 1890s and 1970s in South Asia.

The geography of the territory where Abdul Ghaffar Khan's reform work
took place is essential for an understanding of its importance. The region
where the Pakhtuns – his people – lived was particularly rugged and moun-
tainous. This environmental condition had caused a split of Pakhtun society
into two main groups (which were in turn subdivided according to their
ethnic identities), between the tribal groups of the mountains and those settled
in the plains (Hussain 2000: 8–17). These territorial features prevented this
border area from ever coming entirely under the control of any government –
including the British government – and it remained under the control of its
indigenous people, the only ones capable of administering the area.

Precisely for these reasons and for the geo-strategic importance that the
Khyber Pass had for controlling India, the British always treated the
North-West Frontier Province of India in a "special way":

> As stated earlier, because of its distinctive character, the province was
> treated by the British in a "special way." Security considerations were
> given priority over social, economic and political reforms. Unlike other
> provinces of British India, where reforms were introduced, the N-WFP
> [the North-West Frontier Province] was neglected and intentionally
> governed through "Special Ordinances," Frontier Crimes Regulations
> (FCR) being one amongst them. Interestingly, after the departure of the
> British from the subcontinent, still this draconian law continued to exist
> in the tribal areas of the N-WFP. The main aim of the colonial
> government in impeding the pace of reforms was to discourage the
> local inhabitants from undermining the status quo for their province.
>
> (Shah 2007: 87)

The repercussions of this "special treatment" were also manifest in the
backwardness of the schooling process that in the North-West Frontier
Province were still entrusted to the Koranic schools, given the absence of
government schools. For this reason, Abdul Ghaffar Khan began his work
of social reform as an educator, creating new schools that in addition to
religious teachings tried to instil a national identity.

From his youth, Abdul Ghaffar Khan began to approach nonviolence by
rejecting the deeply ingrained code of honor of the Pakhtun people, "one of
the most violent peoples of the earth" (Easwaran 2008: 24). His efforts to
convince them to abandon the use of force and recourse to blood vendetta
(*badai*) for any murder or insult suffered by one's ethnic group or family,
occupied his entire life and even led him to realize a project that Gandhi
himself had dreamed of but had failed to fulfill: the creation of the first

nonviolent army in history, the "servants of God" (*khudai khidmatgar*), which opposed the British nonviolently, devotionally and courageously.

It must be emphasized that Abdul Ghaffar Khan's brand of nonviolence, despite being influenced in his mature period by Gandhi's message, originated well before he knew Gandhi and was characterized by a profound knowledge of the Koran and a profound internalization of its message of peace. According to this vision, the Koran indicates the situations in which the use of violence is admissible, but it is a matter of dictates aimed at protocoling the use of force with precise rules, condemning aggression and a disproportionate use of violence in terms of the damage suffered. In this vision, the use of force was merely a defensive and not offensive mechanism. This is a precept expressed several times in the Koran and contained in the Sura of the Bees where the adherent of faith is urged to moderation, forgiveness and tolerance: "if you punish, do so to the degree of the wrong suffered. If you endure patiently, this will be [even] better for those who have been patient" (Piccardo 2009: 241).

From the viewpoint of a moderate of the Koran it serves to recall that war also obeyed the precise rules contained in the Sunna of the Envoy, which acknowledged the legitimacy of a purely defensive war in which belligerence was a temporary exception to be concluded as soon as possible. Military actions were also regulated by a clear code of ethics which prescribed that prisoners be treated humanely, receiving the same treatment as Muslim fighters, and not be subjected to torture to extract information. Neither may homes be destroyed, waters polluted, trees cut down or animals killed.

These are pronouncements that inevitably refer to the problem of *jihad* and how it is interpreted in the Western and in the Muslim world. The view Abdul Ghaffar Khan embraced distinguished between two types of *jihad*: the *minor jihad*, which concerned military commitment to defend oneself or to enforce one's rights (if injured or seriously maltreated by oppressors or tyrants), and the more important *major jihad* or *Jihad fi sanbil Allah*, which means "committing oneself to the way of God" without any warlike or aggressive content. "Any behavior that goes beyond what is obligatory and prescribed, in ritual practice, work, study or social commitment, can be considered *jihad* whenever the effort produced tends to please Allah and the vision of His Countenance" (Piccardo 2009: 583). It was an effort "that implies a harmonious existence, an evolution of the self, an overcoming of one's weaknesses, an application of divine dictates" (Easwaran 2008: 9).

And the problem of proselytism linked to *jihad* was precisely one of the prime experiences of Ghaffar Khan's childhood. Ghaffar Khan was only 7 years old when, in 1897, Mullah Mastun began to preach *jihad*, a holy war that should drive out the British and restore Delhi to Islam. It was a radical interpretation of the precept contained in the Koran and that could be put to work to achieve independence from the British. The result was a bloody revolt in which the Pakhtuns, armed with knives and old muskets, held in check for hours British troops armed with cannons, mines and breech-loading rifles. The deadlock was broken only with the arrival of a new British contingent. The retaliation was fierce. A contingent of 35,000 men and 60 cannons was organized, which scoured the valley's villages, plundering all their transportable farm produce and valuables. What could not be carried away was burned. The valley of Tirah was made a desert while in the mountains children and the elderly died of cold and hunger. The episode shocked Abdul Ghaffar Khan with a lasting impression of the consequences of hatred and resentment on both sides.

Between 1907 and 1909 Khan was the second boy in the village to study in an English institution (the first was his elder brother). The experience inspired him to work within the educational system and organize his own schools, a project that went hand in hand with his approach to farm work, meeting the backwardness and ignorance of the common people. This enabled him to understand the importance of scholastic training for achieving true social change and improving the living conditions of the poorest segments of the population. It was then that he decided the time had come to serve, and he would do so by attempting to guarantee a minimum education to all.

In 1910 he founded his first school, which was an immediate success because it turned out to be the first and only alternative to English schools. The experience encouraged him to organize several others with the help of Haij Shaeb, an activity that aroused the concern of the British, who felt they were losing control of the basic aspect of human life and socialization that education represented.

During the First World War Abdul Ghaffar Khan visited a vast number of villages and established schools wherever possible, in the belief that

> the Pathans hate compulsion and dictation of any type, but by their own free will, they are prepared to work in unity and cooperation with others in this country as well as their brethren of the tribal territories, who have so long been kept aloof from us and forced to have a life unworthy of a people. But while I share these sentiments with my people, I cannot for a moment deny them the right of self-determination.
>
> (Khan 2010: 4)

It was at this time that people began to see him as a guide for their emancipation because of his nonviolent defiance of British authority, giving him the nickname of *Badshah Khan*, which meant "Khan of Khan," "King of Kings."

In 1919, with the repeal of the Rowlatt Act, according to which India had to remain subject to a regime of restrictive rights and freedoms that had been introduced during the First World War, Gandhi's first *satyagraha* for independence began.

In the Frontier, Khan, who urged resistance, was arrested for the first time and sentenced without trial to six months in prison. His leg irons were so tight for his build that they wore away the flesh of his ankles to the bone, causing him permanent injuries. Meanwhile, the village of Utmanzai was surrounded by the army and its inhabitants (without regard for the aged, women and children) were crowded into the yard of the school Khan had founded, where soldiers aimed their weapons at them, as if they were about to shoot, while others looted and vandalized the town (Easwaran 2008: 86–87).

In 1920, on the occasion of the historic session of the Indian National Congress, Badshah was able to approach Gandhi for the first time, but on his return to Utmanzai was again thrown into prison with a three-year sentence of forced labor for attempting to educate his people.

When he was released from prison in 1923, he set up the Youth League (*Pakhtun Jirga*) and launched a new series of reforms hailed by the liberal press. One of these was his own magazine, the *Pakhtun* (or *The Pathan*), which challenged the *purdah*, the practice that prevented women from actively participating in social life. Women were encouraged to leave their homes and become active in defending Ghaffar Khan's pacifist, nonviolent movement. They went throughout the frontier districts, giving speeches, presenting their ideas and teaching what they had learned. But in the arch-conservative North-West Frontier Province such activities were considered scandalous:

> One of the characteristics of the Pakhtun society was to give top priority to avenge murder of a blood relative; the educated segment equally approved of this practice. Women were debarred from inheritance and had very little access to educational institutions. It was considered enough for them to be able to recite the Holy Koran and to know how to offer prayers five times a day. They hardly had a say in choosing their spouse and making of other choices regarding their lives. In fact, women in the Pakhtun society like in any other primordial society were considered private property. Men were, and are, responsible for looking after them as they would take care of their other property. In those days fighting and farming were two main preoccupations of the Pakhtuns and modem education was considered a passport to Hell by the religious minded, and getting religious education had no place in the priorities of the upper and ultramodern strata of the society.
>
> (Rauf 2006: 38)

At that time, besides India, Palestine, Lebanon, Syria and Iran were also in turmoil. Islamic countries were undergoing modernizing reforms. Islam was in a moment of rebirth.

However, Khan's most original and interesting contribution to the liberation struggle was the creation, in 1929, of the *khudai khidmatgar*, the "servants of God," the first completely nonviolent professional army in history. The members were Pakhtuns converted to nonviolence who, wearing distinctive red shirts, went into the villages to serve and support projects for social improvement, such as opening new schools, maintaining order and preaching against the *badai*.

> One who aspired to become a Khudai Khidmatgar, declared on solemn oath: "I am a Khudai Khidmatgar, and as God needs no service I shall serve Him by serving His creatures selflessly. I shall never use violence, I shall not retaliate or take revenge, and I shall forgive anyone who indulges in oppression and excesses against me. I shall not be a party to any intrigue, family feudus [*sic*, feuds] and enmity, and I shall treat every Pakhtun as my brother and comrade. I shall give up evil customs and practices. I shall lead a simple life, do good and refrain from wrong-doing. I shall develop good character and cultivate good habits. I shall not lead any idle life. I shall expect no reward for my services. I shall be fearless and be prepared."
>
> (Khan 2010: 14–15)

When in 1930 Gandhi began his Salt March that ended in Dandi with the collection of a handful of sea salt and the breaking of the British monopoly on that precious good, all of India, including Abdul Ghaffar Khan, wanted to support the initiative by organizing a meeting at Utmanzai, but he was arrested and sentenced to three years in prison. But the British had underestimated the support Khan had from the Frontier population, which soon gathered in Kissa Khani bazaar to protest in a strictly nonviolent manner against the provision.

It was one of the most tragic moments of the entire Frontier struggle for India's independence. The British police fired on and brutally killed many people. The entire platoon responsible for the carnage was arrested and seventeen men court-martialed and harshly condemned:

> The nonviolent movement won the love, affection and sympathy of the people. It generated in the Pakhtuns a spirit of patriotism and brotherhood and brought about a great revolution in their poetry, literature and way of loving.
>
> (Khan 2010: 26)

After these events the *khudai khidmatgar* were outlawed and persecuted. Their headquarters were destroyed, and their red shirts seized. It was clear that the British feared more the nonviolent Pakhtuns, who preferred to die for their homeland rather than break their vow of nonviolence made to God, than they did violent ones.

At the end of 1930, Lord Irwin invited Gandhi to Delhi to negotiate a truce. For the first time the British recognized Gandhi as a leader of a movement and his right to represent Indians aroused in protest. After days of negotiations, Gandhi and Irwin signed a peer negotiation in which civil disobedience was suspended and political prisoners were released throughout India. In the Frontier, Khan's movement obtained some long-term concessions from the government (Easwaran 2008: 130–31).

In this period Badshah Khan's beliefs led him to embrace vegetarianism to internalize to the fullest extent Muhammad's message to show compassion for animals and in the Hadith had written that Allah had suggested to him: "if you really must kill, instead of 40 chickens you kill a goat, instead of 40 goats kill 10 cows, instead of 40 cows kill 10 camels" (Easwaran 2008: 15) because the life of every creature had value, and as many as possible must be preserved. Khan also embraced the importance Gandhi attributed to the manufacture of clothes and began dressing with fabrics sewn by himself. He also left his lands in the care of his children.

The British feared the fame of this Pakhtun who roamed unarmed over the Frontier, preaching love, nonviolence and the emancipation of women:

> in the holy Koran you are treated on an equal footing with men. Today you are oppressed because we men have ignored the commandments of God and the Prophet. Today we follow custom and hold you in subjection. But thanks to God we have understood that victories and defeats, progress and setbacks are as common for you as for us.
>
> (Easwaran 2008: 135)

The authorities began to have him followed, and the British press began to describe him as a crude Islamic extremist to create a negative image of him in the eyes of the public. This caused Ghaffar Khan to be arrested again along with his older brother, Dr. Khan Saheb. For three years, Abdul Ghaffar Khan was held without trial in isolation, unable to communicate or receive any kind of information from the outside. Released with his brother in 1934, he went to the Congress of Bombay with Gandhi, where he rejected the offer of the presidency.

A few days later he was again incarcerated for uttering seditious comments. He spent two years in prison, in isolation and without a bed.

Released in 1936 and banned from the Frontier, he lived for a few years in Gandhi's ashram. In 1937 he succeeded in obtaining the very important result of self-government in his region, while in the first Frontier elections his brother was elected prime minister. With the powers now attributed to him, Khan Saheb managed to overturn the provision that had hitherto prevented his brother from returning home.

On his return home, Ghaffar Khan, accompanied by Gandhi, was greeted by crowds of exultant red shirts. The occasion was important for Gandhi, who showed great interest in the *khudai khidmatgar*. In India the Pathans were considered a harsh, proud people who aroused terror in children, but the *khudai khidmatgar* had been able to tame their pride and vengefulness to serve their nation in a totally nonviolent way.

Ghaffar Khan's example and his steadfastness and social commitment had converted one of the most violent nations in the world. And this had come about simply through interaction.

> The sociologist Georg Simmel wrote about the importance of the valence of interactions, whether they are positive or negative, as well as such factors as their intensity and the amount of the self that is involved, which is basically an identity issue. One might also think about the valence of conflicts and identity issues in analyzing Badshah Khan's contribution to our understanding of violence, nonviolence, and the relationship between the two. If the lore about the Pathans was true – and there is some evidence to suggest it was, to some extent – then it is significant that the intensity of the "Kudhai Kidtmatgar's" nonviolence was proportionate to the legendary Pathan violence.
>
> (Kurtz 2011: 250)

Despite the friendship between Hindus and Muslims represented by the fraternal collaboration of the "two Gandhis," events prevented India from being united. Although the Indian National Congress strove for independence from Britain and national unity, the Muslim League (which until then had collaborated with the colonizers and called for the Empire's dominion status), from 1940 on, through Alì Jinnah, it began to demand the creation of a separate Islamic state that would take the name of Pakistan.

Both Gandhi and Badshah Khan rejected the separatist idea and attempted to contain the clashes caused by the intolerance fomented by radicalism in the regions of Noakhali, Bihar and Punjab in the period of transition that would lead to independence. But in the end the Congress had to resign itself to the birth of two states. Which is what took place in 1947.

Badshah Khan, who till then had fought alongside the Hindus, felt abandoned and disappointed now that Pakistan had come into being. Nonetheless, he accepted the new situation and began to urge for recognition of the existence of Pakhtunistan, with a Pakhtun government for Pakhtuns, in a project that would allow all the major provinces of Pakistan to have their own semi-autonomous provinces, such as the Bengalis in Bengal, the Sindis in Sind, the Punjabis in Punjab, and the Beluchis in Beluchistan.

After stating these requests, he was again imprisoned. Of the first thirty years of Pakistan's existence, he spent fifteen in prison and seven in exile (Easwaran 2008: 187). He died in Peshawar in 1988, at the age of 95. It is useful to remember Ghaffar Khan even today, in order not to forget the man who for the first time transformed the concept of *jihad* into a nonviolent movement aimed at eliminating social and political injustices. Unlike Gandhi, whose nonviolence was strongly based on ethico-philosophical principles, Ghaffar Khan's nonviolence and pacifism were decidedly pragmatic. For him the adherent's acts aimed not only at truth and justice, but also and above all at social well-being. As David Cortright (2008: 190–91) observes, it is impossible for a Muslim to practice his faith without a parallel social commitment. The concept of withdrawal from the concerns of society has no logical place in moderate Islam. Rather, society is where *jihad* (understood as an inner effort towards God) should be realized and where individuals can realize their potential (Said *et al.* 2001: 7).

Although the Koran, the Sunna and the Hadith admit the use of force, and although many Islamic groups have appealed to precepts such as "Kill the idolaters wherever you find them, and capture them, and blockade them, and watch for them at every lookout" (Piccardo 2009: 168) or "O Prophet! Strive against the disbelievers and the hypocrites and be stern with them" to justify wars of a political nature, many Islamic scholars have rejected this concept of holy war as an error:

> They point to the cardinal principle in the Koran that "there can be no compulsion in religion." On this point the Koran is unequivocal: "The truth is from your Lord; believe it if you like, or do not." The message to non-Muslims is, "To you your religion to me mine." These passages counsel tolerance and patience toward other faiths and in no way provide justification for religious war.
>
> (Cortright 2008: 192)

As previously mentioned, the Koran places limits on the use of force, which is permitted only for defensive purposes.

There is no doubt that Ghaffar Khan internalized these messages of tolerance, nonviolence, and peace as a service to others, and attempted to demonstrate concretely how to realize his religious message. Since he was predominantly a man of action who never set down his thought in any coherent written form, it is difficult for us to translate it into a systematic philosophy. For this reason, it is really important to understand its history.

## Notes

1 To understand the comparison between Pauline love and *ahimsa*, it suffices to read Saint Paul's First Letter to the Corinthians: "If I speak in the tongues of men and of angels, but have not love, I am a noisy gong or a clanging cymbal. And if I have prophetic powers, and understand all mysteries and all knowledge, and if I have all faith, so as to remove mountains, but have not love, I am nothing. If I give away all I have, and if I deliver up my body to be burned, but have not love, I gain nothing. Love is patient and kind; love does not envy or boast; it is not arrogant or rude. It does not insist on its own way; it is not irritable or resentful; it does not rejoice at wrongdoing, but rejoices with the truth. Love bears all things, believes all things, hopes all things, endures all things. Love never ends. As for prophecies, they will pass away; as for tongues, they will cease; as for knowledge, it will pass away. For we know in part and we prophesy in part, but when the perfect comes, the partial will pass away. When I was a child, I spoke like a child, I thought like a child, I reasoned like a child. When I became a man, I gave up childish ways. For now we see in a mirror dimly, but then face to face. Now I know in part; then I shall know fully, even as I have been fully known. So now faith, hope, and love abide, these three; but the greatest of these is love."

2 Clifford argued that this edict of the British parliament provided funds for sectarian education in voluntary elementary schools owned by the Church of England and Roman Catholics. For this reason, he formed the National Passive Resistance Committee with the aim of convincing other nonconformists to stop paying taxes until the edict was repealed.

## References

Bobbio, N. (2007) Pacifismo. In Bobbio, N., Matteucci, N., and Pasquino, G., eds., *Dizionario di Politica*. Torino: Utet.

Cebi, S. S. (2011) Conservative parties. In Kurian, G. T., ed., *The Encyclopedia of Political Science*. Washington, DC: CQ Press.

Cortright, D. (2008) *Peace: A History of Movements and Ideas*. New York: Cambridge University Press.

Easwaran, E. (2008) *Badshah Khan, Il Gandhi Musulmano*. Casale Monferrato: Sonda.

Gandhi, M. K. (1963) *Antiche come le montagne*. Milano: Edizioni di Comunità.

Gandhi, M. K. (1996) *Teoria e pratica della non-violenza*. Torino: Einaudi.

Gandhi, M. K. (2010) *Il mio credo, il mio pensiero*. Rome: Newton Compton Editori.

Garrard, G. (2011) Enlightenment political thought. In Kurian, G. T., ed., *The Encyclopendia of Political Science*. Washington, DC: CQ Press.

Hussain, S. I. (2000) *Some Major Pukhtoon Tribes along the Pak–Afghan Border.* Peshawar: Area Study Center, Peshawar, and Hanns Seidel Foundation.

Kant, I. (1903) *Perpetual Peace: A Philosophical Essay.* London: Swan Sonnenschein & Co.

Khan, A. G. (2010) *Words of Freedom, Ideas of a Nation: Abdul Ghaffar Khan.* New Delhi: Penguin Books India.

Kurtz, L. R. (2011) Peace profile: Abdul Ghaffar Khan's nonviolent jihad. *Peace Review* 23(2), 245–251.

Losurdo, D. (2010) *La non-violenza, una storia fuori dal mito.* Bari: Editori Laterza.

Piccardo, H. R. (2009) *Il Corano.* Rome: Newton Compton Editori.

Pontara, G. (1965) The rejection of violence in Gandhian ethics of conflict resolution. *Journal of Peace Research* 2(3), 197–214.

Pontara, G. (2007) Gandhismo. In Bobbio, N., Matteucci, N., and Pasquino, G., eds., *Il Dizionario di Politica.* Torino: Utet.

Rauf, A. (2006) Socio-educational reform movements in N.W.F.P.: a case study of Anjuman-i-Islahul Afaghina. *Pakistan Journal of History & Culture* 27(2): 31–60.

Said, A. A., Funk, N. C., and Kadayifici, A. S. (2001) Introduction: Islamic approaches to peace and conflict resolution. In Said, A. A., Funk, N. C., and Kadayifici, A. S., eds., *Peace and Conflict Resolution in Islam: Precept and Practice.* Lanham: University Press of America.

Shah, S. W. A. (2007) Abdul Ghaffar Khan, the *Khudai Khidmatgars*, Congress and the partition of India. *Pakistan Vision* 8(2), 86–115.

Thoreau, H. D. (1866) *A Yankee in Canada with Anti-slavery and Reform Papers.* Boston: Ticknor and Fields.

Valverde, M. (2017) *Michel Foucault.* Abingdon: Taylor & Francis.

Voltaire (2006) *Trattato sulla tolleranza.* Milano: Feltrinelli.

Walters, R. G. (1997) *American Reformers: 1815–1860.* New York: Hill & Wang.

# 2 The European pathway to peace

## Peace traditions during the world wars

As became clear from Chapter 1, the first activities and associations aimed at resisting the choices of unjust governments and seeking ethico-philosophical bases for a universal peace can be traced to religious arguments linked principally to the Christian tradition and later, with Gandhi, also to the Hindu tradition. However, it is incorrect to think that the pacifist experience was limited to moral, individual and natural-law arguments. In late modern and contemporary history, various pacifist tendencies have cropped up sporadically in response to historico-political contingencies, and for this reason European and Western pacifist movements are characteristically "social formation[s] fundamentally concerned with the problems of war, militarism, conscription, mass violence, and ideas of internationalism, globalism, and non-violent relations between people" (Young 1986: 185). These are trends that, since the 1950s, have developed in relation to the gap between the South and the North of the world: issues such as hunger, poverty, sustainable development, democracy and civil rights (see Carter 1992).

For the purposes of this discussion, we will group all these tendencies into three distinct macro-trends or macro-forms of pacifism, according to the different ways in which they explain the origin of wars or the means they employ to eliminate them: ethico-religious pacifism, internationalist pacifism, and socialist pacifism. The ethico-religious pacifism that was treated in the first chapter continued to play an extremely important role in the further development of pacifist ideas in the religious realm. Examples of this are the American Society of Friends (Quakers) and the pacifist Catholic movement Pax Christi, first established in France and later throughout Europe.

Internationalist, liberal or economic pacifism

held that the main cause of wars was economic protectionism, which forced states to obtain through conquest what they could not obtain through free trade: Cobden's idea that through the liberation of economic frontiers merchants would gradually replace warriors went hand in hand with Spencer's philosophy of history, by which the fatal laws of evolution would transform ancient warlike and war-waging societies into peaceful industrial societies.

(Bobbio 2004: 664)

Murder and destruction were conceived as an ethical argument against war and, referring to Bentham (1823: vi), the exponents of international pacifism claimed that "it is the greatest happiness of the greatest number that is the measure of right and wrong." Unlike ethico-religious pacifism, the internationalist variety aimed at avoiding war while not totally renouncing the use of violence, an aspect that did not surface until 1914, when internationalist pacifist movements were divided into two opposite poles: those who believed in absolute pacifism and those who were willing to support war in most cases.

What narrowed the successes that internationalism might have had was the emergence of Europe's nation states and the development of totalitarianism, militarism and the onrush of imperialist expansionism. Nevertheless, there is no doubt about the contribution that this pacifist tendency made to creating international referee institutions able to exploit the tools of global capitalism in order to favor a reduction of conflicts at the European and worldwide level:

The liberal internationalists had formed the International Peace Bureau (1892), associated with the great peace conferences at The Hague, and agitated for the League of Nations (after 1920, supporting it through the League of Nations Unions). They also stressed civilian democratic control of the war (via the Union of Democratic Control in Britain) with protection of civil liberties, as against military autocracy.

(Young 1986: 191)

Lastly, there was socialist pacifism, which recognized the need for worldwide social change in response to the problems of injustice, economic disparities and political repression. This tendency, however, was divided into two main currents: "socialist war resistance" and "socialist internationalism."

Socialist war resistance opposed "militarist governments, conscription and war preparations, which they perceived to be integral aspects of capitalism, imperialism and class rule" (Young 1986: 194) and was fostered by people of a non-Marxist socialist ilk: trade unionists and anarchists who transformed movements in favor of eliminating compulsory conscription into an authentic pacifist movement. Both before and after 1914, movements against compulsory conscription, strikes and mass mobilizations emerged throughout Europe. The dream of these socialist initiatives was to be able to set up an international workers' mobilization to reject war as an instrument of imperialism, while not giving up their aspirations for a proletarian revolution.

Socialist pacifism thus remained divided between its two souls: on the one hand, the rejection of militarism as an instrument of bourgeois capitalism, and on the other, the support for militarism linked to the dream of a violent revolution by the working class that would lead it to subvert power relations within society. This second strand found expression in the Socialist International, an organization that was by no means popular, made up of the leaders of socialist states and organizations that remained very much rooted in the national issues of their members. This was why most of the European socialist parties in 1914 adhered to the call to arms in order to preserve the territorial unity of the states to which they belonged. Preserving the revolution was considered an even higher goal than preserving peace.

During recent history, social movements linked to pacifism have had various phases usually characterized by being more hectic on the eve of conflict, losing importance during war and re-emerging in the post-war period. From the late nineteenth to the early twentieth century, peace talks and projects increased in number and importance to meet the need for the stability of nation states and to respond to the social transformations under way in those years.

For example, in 1898 the Tsar of Russia Nicholas II promoted an international peace conference in favor of disarmament, which was held at The Hague in 1899 and renewed in 1907. The first Peace Conference produced three conventions on the law of war, three declarations on prohibiting recourse to certain military means in wartime, and laid the foundations for the establishment of a Permanent Court of Arbitration. The second Peace Conference aimed at reinforcing and integrating the decisions made during the first one and produced a declaration and thirteen conventions (eight of them exclusively on war law) (Mancini 2009: 25–26).

The nation states' commitment to peace – which in that period was also favored by some socialist movements of the Second International – was hastily set aside at the outbreak of the First World War, decreeing the defeat of pacifist ideals. Yet this defeat, combined with the death and destruction caused by total war, subsequently reignited the interactional debate on the establishment of a system of international norms and institutions to regulate conflicts between states. The influence of these debates is also evident in the vision of the American President Woodrow Wilson, as highlighted in the Fourteen Points he illustrated to the United States Congress on 8 January

1918. In particular, the fourteenth declaration of intent provided for the formation of an Association of Nations that would stipulate for states mutual guarantees of independence and territorial integrity.

These peace plans were the fertile terrain on which the peace talks of 1918 took place and from which the 1919 Versailles Treaty and the League of Nations came about, the purpose of the latter being to guarantee international peace and security by fostering cooperation between nations.

When these very important goals were reached, the importance of pacifist movements and ideals again seemed to diminish. This was also due to the choice of the United States to pursue an isolationist policy by not adhering to the very League of Nations that Wilson himself had envisioned. It was a choice that already foretold the future failure of the League, which not only was born "lame" of one of its main promoters, but also presented normative choices (power of veto, non-permanent assembly, absence of armed forces) that made it powerless to prevent the outbreak of new conflicts.

In the belief that economic inequalities were at the root of conflicts, the European pacifist movements began to see increasingly eye-to-eye with the socialists, but the appearance of Nazi fascism, Stalinism and totalitarianism in general led to their radical restraint and to the outbreak of the Second World War. However, during the war religious-based and Christian ethical pacifist ideals continued to be active primarily through organizations advocating conscientious objection:

> [...] during the Second World War, well over 60,000 men and around 1,000 women in Britain took the decision to register as conscientious objectors and claim exemption from military service. They refused to fight or to undertake war-related work as a matter of conscience. They came from different backgrounds and social classes and their reasons for swimming against the national tide of war and militarism also varied. But however different they were, as people, they all shared one basic belief, that it was wrong, whether for religious, moral, political or humanitarian reasons, to be conscripted for war and to take up arms and fight, no matter how great the danger facing Britain, no matter how much pressure was put on them to change their minds.
>
> (Kramer 2013: 3)

The descending arc of the pacifist movements took a sharp upturn starting on 6 August 1945, when the US Air Force dropped the first atomic bomb on Hiroshima (followed three days later by the one dropped on Nagasaki). For the first time, the destruction, deaths and magnitude of the damage caused by the atomic bomb placed humanity before the imminent danger of its very survival (Schell 1982).

Among the first to highlight the dangers of the use of atomic energy were the scientists of the Manhattan Project: Albert Einstein and Robert Oppenheimer. Their calls for peace, humanity and disarmament were followed – between the 1950s and the 1980s – by various waves of political activism in favor of arms control and the end of the Cold War caused between the two opposing blocs of the United States and the Union of Soviet Socialist Republics. The opposition between these blocs had caused in the immediate post-war period a nuclear arms race that made the balance of power more and more unstable and the escalation towards a new total war an ever-greater likelihood.

So, at the same time there were pacifist movements pushing for disarmament and philosophical and political thought immediately following the Second World War oriented toward analyzing the crisis of democratic systems and their warlike drift dictated by the totalitarian threat. One cannot forget Max Weber's sociological analysis of authoritarian institutionalization, charismatic authorities and modern institutional systems, and Hans Kelsen's juridical approach in *Peace through Law* (1944), in which he proposed establishing a World State, conceived in Hobbesian terms as a Leviathan for other Leviathans, and of an international court of justice that could exercise coercion against any state that attacked the world order (Kelsen 2007: 35).

Kelsen's juridical approach was later followed by the Italian philosopher Norberto Bobbio's efforts to expose the criticalities imposed by the legal limits at the basis of the United Nations and to highlight how "peace through law" could be the only practicable path in a world dominated by distrust between opposing blocs.

## The disillusionment of the oppressed in Simone Weil

The themes of nonviolence and peace were also topics especially dear to Simone Weil, who between 1909 and 1943 repeatedly questioned her philosophico-political orientations until she arrived at a mystico-religious viewpoint that led her to convert to Catholicism – which she considered the slave religion par excellence.

The peculiarity of her thought lay in the fact that she was predominantly a woman drawn to action, and for this reason all the information we have comes from diary pages, short essays, personal correspondence and newspaper articles.

In Augusto del Noce's interpretation (1968: 1–56), Simone Weil's life and thought were divisible into three great stages: her agnostic period, characterized by a preponderance of doubt until she encountered Marx; her revolutionary period, which began with her adoption of Marxist theories, which answered the questions posed by her agnostic period; and her gnostic period, in which she approached Plato and the non-Catholic Christian spirituality that led her to conclude that Marx's philosophy had focused on values too distant from mankind, forgetting that we are not just flesh but also Spirit.

Her agnostic phase was strongly influenced by the thought of the pacifist Émile-Auguste Chartier (better known as Alain), her teacher at the Lyceum Henri IV in Paris where she studied between 1925 and 1928. Alain was a secular radical who fervently believed in mankind's freedom to choose between good and evil independently of a transcendent God. For Chartier, God was the universal Spirit that stood beyond the forces of nature and humanity. He was a denial of any form of force, glorifying all that was peace and acceptance.

In Kantian terms, Alain was convinced of the presence of a transcendent being that made the choices of good and evil possible through the hope of a future reward, but he also realized the dual risk of this conviction: on the one hand, the presence of a transcendent being made it almost impossible to fulfill one's duty as such, and on the other, the negation of this transcendence risked leading us adrift towards an always objectionable secularism as harbinger of the cult of worldliness.

The need not to abandon faith but to make it more "human" made Alain humanize God in the figure of the *enfant-dieu*, a fragile deity like the Jesus of the Bethlehem grotto. Not the God of armies or of the Apocalypse, but a humble, poor, weak God devoted to compassion and love for the underdog. Simone Weil was profoundly influenced by this lofty vision of love in the figure of the *enfant-dieu*, the idea of the Virgin Mary as a charitable mother and the image of the Crucified Christ who stood for the culmination of God's love for mankind and the synthesis of the humanization of the transcendent. From Alain, Weil also inherited the position that mankind is at the center of history; a mankind that, through misfortune (*malheur*), came to abandon its ego, synonymous with power and strength, to embrace the impersonal, namely suffering, pain and injustice. "The man who wanted to annul his ego gave up the power he could have had and became a supplicant; he understood that only humility and contempt for himself and the actions he might have accomplished if he were clothed in power were the truth and the reality of existence" (Laurenti 2007: 24): a hero who succeeded in summarizing in himself love and suffering.

Following this line of reasoning and eager to test on herself the effects of the spirit of power, Weil supported trade union struggles, giving up part of her salary to help the poorest and most destitute workers. This choice led her to abandon teaching and work in the Renault factories where she directly experienced the alienation, exploitation and human uprooting of a world in constant evolution no longer on a human scale, where the self was nullified under the impulse of the violence of slavery.

This was the period that Del Noce defined as revolutionary: a period in which Simone let herself be beguiled by the early writings of a Marx not yet associated with economic dogmatism, because in them she felt the tension of justice and truth she had also found in the gospels. She was also fascinated by the idea of socio-political renewal that she encountered in his writings as intrinsic to oppressed peoples, but despite this with time Weil moved away from Marxism and began to denounce its claim to carry out a scientific study of the human condition, in total disregard for any understanding of the Spirit. "Marx's error was that he wanted to develop a rigorous method to contain the whole of reality, thus formulating an inevitably tragic dogmatism" (Laurenti 2007: 63). But even the blind faith in a revolution capable of resolving all the problems afflicting contemporary social reality resulted in an unsustainable thesis in the eyes of a woman who "demanded that there be not the slightest inconsistency between her own convictions and life" (Pétrement 1994: 65).

This awareness of the uselessness of the Marxian revolution, combined with a conception of social progress as the result of the "enlightened goodwill of men acting in an individual capacity" (Weil 2004: 57), gave rise to Weil's pessimism, made up of *malheur* and that sense of rootlessness that, as for Jaffier in *Venise sauvée* ("Venice preserv'd"), made the reality in which she lived seem alien to her.

The abandonment of the philosophy of action characterized what Del Noce defined as the phase of gnosticism in which, through Plato, she was able to direct her attention to the Christian spiritual dimension. In the *Republic* Plato speaks of the fundamental virtue that should pervade all three classes into which the state was divided – artisans, guardians and philosophers – and that was justice. And as for Weil, in Plato the just was the one who suffered so that justice could be carried out, as also in the Parable of the Cave, in which the philosopher sacrifices himself for truth. By tracing a parallel with the Platonic concept of justice, Weil found that the philosopher par excellence was Christ, who having come to know the truth became man and let himself be sacrificed on the cross to transmit his message of love to others.

And precisely the image of the Cross and of the Father's Love were for her a synthesis of the Christian message. The Father was pure love, he who knew how to understand and console us and love us even when we were wicked. An image influenced by Alain of the Virgin Mary and that found its highest expression of love in the Cross: God loved mankind so much that he sacrificed his son and became a victim himself. "The symbolism of the Cross encompassed the highest and deepest meaning of

Love in its truest dimension, and above all free of any form of selfishness and egocentrism" (Laurenti 2007: 76–77).

In 1938, and during the last years of her short life, she cultivated a fruitful friendship with the Dominican Joseph-Marie Perrin, who repeatedly invited Weil to be baptized and embrace the Church, but she refused, preferring to "stay on the threshold" because of her inability to accept the spirit of power inherent in the social institution of the Church, and her refusal to embrace the idea of resurrection. This would mean the passage of mankind to transcendence, while she wanted to remain rooted to suffering and pain. Crossing the threshold and being baptized would have meant denying what she believed in. It was then pain that characterized the third phase of Simone Weil's thought, namely mysticism. It was through suffering – the devastating headaches that afflicted her because of her precarious health – that in 1942, in the Benedictine monastery of Solesmes, she had what she called a mystical experience that enabled her to retrace in Christ's passion on the cross the pains she herself was suffering. It was a very important moment, which led her to confirm her choice to take the side of the outcasts, the underdogs, the sufferers, and immolate herself like Christ on the cross, for the spirit of truth.

Thus, we get a clear picture of the sociological critique that Weil made of modern society and the ideologies of her age:

> The core of Simone Weil's sociology is her functional theory of oppression. The essence of this theory is that oppression results from the subordination of those who execute to those who command, and that those who command do so in the performance of essential social functions. Simone Weil was not an anarchist. She did not think that subordination could ever be removed from the social order. She distinguished between the "subordination of individual caprices to a social order" and a degree of constraint that is physically and morally stultifying.
>
> (Pierce 1962: 514)

What emerges from Weil's writings is her deep conviction that mankind had lost its humanity by living in a world in which nothing was on a human scale and in which there was a clear division and disproportion between body and spirit. In this sense, she saw human history as one of enslavement and the denial of freedom, in which society was a slavery-fabricating machine, an obfuscator of conscience and need.

The capitalist world in which Weil lived promoted a new form of social oppression: enslavement in the name of the function that individuals must perform within the productive system (Pierce 1962: 512–18). It was within this nexus that she focused her will to change society by placing mankind at the center of everything. The individual, for Weil, must cease to be an object of the system and begin to be the supreme, incalculable value of every society, even those that embody Marxist values.

Weil's ethico-philosophical path, as evidenced in the three phases of her revolutionary period, her Platonic-gnostic period and her mystical period, ideally correspond to three different phases of her reflections on peace, war and nonviolence.

The first period was that of pacifism linked to the points of view of the working class, which had its roots in the crisis of values caused by the First World War and the refusal of a significant number of young people to support patriotic and nationalistic ideas – among them also Weil, who years later wrote:

> Present-day society is comparable to an immense machine that ceaselessly seizes men, and whose commands nobody knows; and those who sacrifice themselves for social progress appear to be people who cling to the wheels and transmission belts to try to stop the machine by letting themselves be mangled. But the powerlessness in which one finds oneself at a certain moment, a powerlessness that must never be considered definitive, cannot exempt one from remaining faithful to oneself, nor excuse surrendering to the enemy, whatever form it takes. The prime enemy remains the administrative, law enforcement and military apparatus, by whatever name it is called: fascism, democracy or dictatorship of the proletariat. [...] The worst possible betrayal, under any circumstances, always lies in accepting submission to this apparatus and trampling all human values, in oneself and others, in order to serve it.
>
> (Weil 2005: 39)

Her rejection of bourgeois values and her refusal to support French foreign policy led her to support the signing of the Briand–Kellogg Pact of 1928, whose purpose was to eliminate war as a means for resolving international disputes, and to join a small group of pacifists called La Volonté de Paix (The Will to Peace).

Her real militancy alongside workers' movements and unions started in 1931, when she began teaching evening classes for miners in Le Puy: a choice dictated by the need she felt to be on the side of the oppressed, the same need that led her to experience directly the alienation of factory work and that made her reject war not only as an absolute evil but above all as a plague that struck hardest the poorest and most disadvantaged classes. "Modern war differs absolutely from anything that was indicated by this name under previous regimes. On the one hand, war just prolongs that other conflict which is called competition, and which makes production itself a simple form of struggle for domination; on the other hand, all economic life is currently oriented towards a future war." So, the interdependence of the military, the economy and war "only reproduces the social relations that make up the very structure of the regime, but at a very high level" (Weil 2005: 32).

War, by reinforcing these social, economic and political factors, therefore tended to favor an authoritarian drift even in those countries that did not initially suffer from this evil.

> Marx showed clearly that the modern mode of production is defined by the subordination of workers to working tools, tools belonging to those who do not work, and how competition, knowing no other weapon than the exploitation of workers, becomes the struggle of every boss against his own workers and, ultimately, of the whole class of bosses against the whole class of workers. Likewise, war today is defined as the subordination of combatants to the instruments of combat; and the armaments, the true heroes of modern wars, are on an equal footing with the men consecrated to their service, controlled by those who do not fight. And since this ruling apparatus has no other way of defeating the enemy than by forcing its soldiers to go to their deaths, the war of one state against another state turns into a war of the government and military apparatus against its own army; and war ultimately presents itself as a war waged by the collective state apparatus and its general staffs against all the men of age to bear arms. Her unceasing will to restore dignity to the oppressed led her, in 1934, to make an in-depth study of the problems of factory work and to draw up the most important testimony on working conditions of that period: the *Factory Diary*, a document describing the alienation and retreat into itself that was leading mankind to self-annihilation, to becoming an inanimate object in the service of producing the wealth of others.
>
> (Weil 2002: 11)

But Weil did not limit herself to criticizing war between states; she also argued that the revolutionary war that originated with the French Revolution and was reproduced in the October Revolution was actually the "tomb of revolution" (Weil 2005: 36) and would remain so as long as it continued to be an instrument of state militarization. This dual rejection and her awareness that revolutionary transformations would be ineffectual for improving the conditions of the working class, as in Russia, also led her to maintain a distance from trade unionism, although the issue of worker exploitation remained of primary importance to her.

Like Gandhi, Weil also believed that one could not imagine evaluating war for the ends it pursued while forgetting the means it employed:

> Not that it is better to censure the use of violence in general, as do pure pacifists: war constitutes, in every age, a very precise kind of violence, and before expressing any judgment, one must study its mechanism. The materialistic method involves first of all examining any human fact by taking into account the consequences necessarily entailed by the means employed, rather than the ends pursued. We cannot solve or merely even pose a problem relating to war without having first dismantled the mechanism of military struggle, that is to say, analyzing the social relationships that it implies under certain technical, economic and social conditions.
>
> (Weil 2002: 9)

In 1936, with the outbreak of the Spanish Civil War and the intensification of the risks of a new world war, Weil's attention was channeled to the study of precarious international equilibriums.

On 8 August 1936, Weil enlisted among the ranks of the Spanish Popular Front because she wanted to avoid making the mistake of Gandhi, whose politics of nonviolence in her view appeared "for now as a somewhat hypocritical form of reformism" (Weil 1999: 34). A further clarification of this choice partly contradictory with the total rejection of war (even revolutionary war) was provided in the letter she wrote to Bernanos:

> I don't like war; but, in war, what has always made me more horrified is the condition of those in the rear lines. When I realized that, in spite of my efforts, I couldn't keep from participating morally in this war, that is to desire every day and every hour the victory of one side and the defeat of the other, I told myself that Paris was for me the rear lines, and I took the train to Barcelona with the intention of enlisting.
>
> (Weil 2005: 50)

Because of her clumsiness and physical weakness she was assigned to the kitchens, where on 20 August she suffered serious burns from a pan of boiling oil. She was admitted to the hospital, believing she would return to duty as soon as she was healed, but soon realized that she no longer felt the need to participate in a war which was not – as she had thought at the beginning – one of hungry peasants against landowners and clergy, but a war between Russia, Germany and Italy.

At the end of this experience there began what can be considered Simone Weil's second period of pacifism, her most radical, in which she supported Chamberlain's policy of appeasement, the intent of which was to avoid conflict at any cost, even allowing German hegemony in Europe: a sacrifice that not even the most anti-war British were willing to endure to guarantee peace. In 1939, despite the German invasion of Czechoslovakia, Weil continued to hope for a solution other than armed conflict. She relied on the fact that no one had yet declared war and hoped German occupation would be temporary, since she felt it was impossible to keep an entire population in check by an unrelenting use of force. In this period both she and Gandhi had "the tendency to read modernity as such as an expression of violence and the consequent difficulty in orienting oneself among different forms of violence" (Losurdo 2010: 119).

However, at the outbreak of the Second World War – this is where what we can consider her third period of pacifist thought came into play – her inner crisis led her to review her position and to pursue the destruction of Hitler; "a furrow came to reopen between her and Gandhi. Again, as in the initial phase of the Spanish war, it was no longer permissible to remain 'in the rear' and she undertook to set up and direct a 'front-line nursing' corps ready to show 'a spirit of total sacrifice'" (Losurdo 2010: 119). To do so she had to abandon the collaborationist France of Marshal Pétain and go to London where De Gaulle was organizing the Resistance, but as it had become impossible to reach England directly, she sailed from Marseilles with her family to go to Casablanca, and from there to New York. Once in New York, haunted by guilt and anxiety, she did her utmost to reach London. Her distance from the suffering of the French people made her feel guilty and filled her with horror. Her anxieties were undiminished even by her project for training front-line nurses, because De Gaulle never consented to its realization.

She was helped by one of her old schoolmates, Maurice Shumann, and finally managed to reach England, where she began to collaborate with France Libre's Office of the Interior with the intention of being sent home with some practical mission. She was greatly disappointed when this turned out to be impossible, and she could not forgive herself for having fled from France. Consequently, she began to eat less and less in an attempt to consume the same quantities of food that were allowed by the rationing imposed on the French at home. She fell ill with tuberculosis, an illness that could have been cured but that became lethal due to malnutrition. She died on 24 August 1943.

From her London period there is a never-published article titled "This War Is a War of Religion," in which she severely criticized the idolatry of modern totalitarianism. For her, the idolatry of totalitarianism was a religious fact that involved the worship of a social reality, in which the idea of opposition between good and evil had no right to enter. When mankind became part of this religion, it evaded the dualism between good and evil, for the very belief in this type of idolatry created a compartmentalization of society that lay beyond the traditional distinction between good and evil by placing itself totally at the service of power:

> In single-party countries, a member of the party who has abdicated once and for all from every quality other than this is no longer subject to sin. He can be clumsy, like a maid who breaks a plate, but whatever he does, he cannot do any harm, because he is exclusively a member of a group – the Party, the Nation – that cannot do any harm.
> (Weil 2005: 124–25)

This false religiosity which in that period had pervaded the whole of Western society, and which replaced the authentic one of Christianity, had to be eradicated and fought to avoid the total annihilation of the identity of peoples and individuals. In this sense, and only in this sense, could war be considered a necessary evil. Here then is explained the seemingly contradictory reasoning on behalf of Weil's activism in support of the war against the Germans that she considered to be a necessary evil to free the West from National Socialist idolatry.

In a world governed by force, mankind has the right and the duty to flee from evil so as not to become a "corpse." In fact, in the essay "Iliad or the Poem of Force," written between 1939 and 1941, Weil argued that "force is what makes anyone subject to it a thing. When it is practiced to an extreme, it makes man a thing, in the most literal sense of the word, because it transforms him into a corpse" (Weil 1974: 11), and not only those who perish from its brutality, but also those who survive and who "are alive, have a soul but nonetheless are a thing" (Weil 1974: 13). Precisely in order to prevent a mankind subjected to idolatry and force from becoming definitively a thing, she admits resorting to war in the case of Nazi fascism and totalitarianism of this kind, since not to resort to this means would be an even greater evil than that caused by war.

## Aldo Capitini's philosophy of the socio-religious change towards omnicracy

An important contribution to the movement for nonviolence was made in Italy by Aldo Capitini (1899–1968), who interiorized Gandhi's teachings and attempted to spread them in Italy. His incessant efforts to raise awareness there achieved the distinction of an authentic socio-political theory (Drago 2007: 265–95).

The son of a municipal employee and a seamstress, he began to study literature on his own and, on entering the Scuola Normale Superiore, also philosophy. In the years that fascism flourished he was an individual of steadfast principles and for this reason he always refused any form of alignment. Disappointed and embittered by the Concordat with the Roman Catholic Church of 1929[1] – a Church that "if it had wanted, by displaying a firm non-cooperation, would have made fascism fall in the space of a week" – realized that "if there is one thing we owe to the fascist period, it is to have clarified definitively that religion is something other than the institution of Roman Catholicism" (Capitini 1960: 33–34). The event was a turning point in Capitini's thought, for from that moment he considered the Catholic Church an obdurate ally of all fascist ideologies (Petricioli and Cherubini 2007: 462).

His opposition to fascism led him to have dealings with individuals who were in the cross hairs of the Black Shirts, and in 1933 to lose the position of economic secretary at the Scuola Normale Superiore (then under the direction of the "philosopher of Fascism" Giovanni Gentile):

> In 1933, he was asked by the president of the Scuola Normale Superiore (the celebrated philosopher Giovanni Gentile) to enroll in the Fascist Party, but being inspired by Gandhi, he refused. He and his friends considered his action to be nonviolent. This marked the birth of active nonviolence in Europe. As a consequence of his refusal, he was expelled from the School.
>
> (Drago 2014: 434)

The essential feature of Capitini's nonviolence was a politico-religious faith in nonviolent social change intent on strengthening the tie between ethics and religion. Although he did not belong to any current or political party, his primary objective was to promote political, social and institutional reform through purely ethical acts. In this sense, together with the philosopher Guido Calogero, he was among the theorists of liberal socialism and the Action Party, which subsequently Norberto Bobbio and many other anti-fascist intellectuals of the time joined, but which Capitini refused to adhere to in order to remain a liberal socialist and an "independent leftist," a term he coined to indicate that the social change he intended to make was not just political but also in part religious (Mencaroni 1999: 3). Unlike Calogero, for whom liberal socialism was transmuted into Actionism, for Capitini it continued to be primarily a "socio-religious orientation" (Parodi 2012: 348).

Still in stark contrast to fascism, in 1944 he established the Social Orientation Centers or COS (Centri di Orientamento Sociale) with the aim of promoting the more active participation of ordinary people in the political and social life of the country. Ideally, the COS were the starting point for realizing what he called *omnicrazia* (omnicracy), namely an advanced and open, grass-roots form of democracy in which everyone should have a public say, without distinction of gender, age, race, nationality, education, status, political party, or any other limitation.

Capitini continued to remain outside the parties and eventually was in large part marginalized from political life. Despite this he continued to be socially active through his awareness-raising initiatives regarding nonviolence (such as his support of Pietro Pinna for recognizing the right to conscientious objection) and religious reform, as with the Centers for Religious Orientation (Centri di Orientamento Religioso), which he founded in 1952 with the aim of promoting dialogue on religions without social or religious constraints (Drago 2014: 437). The social and political reform work that Capitini was carrying out in central and northern Italy was a great inspiration for his sociologist friend Danilo Dolci (whom we will come to in the following pages), who in those years was undertaking his own nonviolent struggle to redevelop the backward areas of the Palermo hinterland (Barone and Mazzi 2008).

In 1955 Capitini published *Religione aperta* (Open religion) but the work was immediately placed on the Index by the Holy Office. Capitini responded to this act of narrow-mindedness by publishing in 1957 a book entitled *Discuto la religione di Pio XII* (I discuss the religion of Pius XII), which was also placed on the Index. Later, in 1961, inspired by the no-nukes Aldermaston Marches in England, Capitini announced the first Peace March from Perugia to Assisi, an event that was very successful and that still takes place at two-year intervals.

For a summary of his thought, first, we must mention that Capitini was very much influenced by his classical studies. In particular, in Foscolo he admired a man who "does not yield to vice, does not yield to tyrants, does not yield to the rowdy mob, and become a statue" (Capitini 1942: 32), and yet he upheld a contemplative and pessimistic historicism. By contrast, in Manzoni he loved the immersion in family life, traditions, religion, the Catholic feasts and his linking of them to cultural expression. As regards Leopardi, he loved to define himself as Kantian–Leopardian, specifying that he had been Kantian even before he encountered Kant. He defined himself as Leopardian because his religious spirit urged him to address not only the living but also the dead in a continuous tension beyond reality, towards a co-presence of the living and the dead. But Leopardi was "a Romantic and his limits are those of Romanticism, in which pain and death are, while present, not redeemed, participated in but not rehabilitated, suffered but not resolved" (Bobbio 2011: 24–25).

Like many intellectuals of his time, Capitini had been influenced by idealism, whose immanentism he preserved, thus rejecting the old vision of an other-worldly God to pray to and worship, and by historicism or attention to mankind as creator of history, though he never came to reject being either idealist or historicist. He even came to "dualize immanence" (Capitini 1947: 19) with a conception of God which was no longer other-worldly but present in everything: a vision that did not negate the quest for the infinite present in the old dualism and that placed humanity at the center of history without becoming a philosophy of self-gratification.

At a time when Italian philosophical interest was almost exclusively focused on Hegelian thought, a thought shut in on itself in a continuous alternation of theses, antitheses and syntheses, Capitini focused his interest on Kant and on the "tension towards the ideal, which is the true, even if unreachable, reality" (Bobbio 2011: 26), an ideal vision for those who did not want to stop to contemplate reality but intended to transform it incrementally, through "addition" (*aggiunta*, Capitini's term for the addition of the religious dimension to politics, transforming political action and ideas, and religion itself; Petricioli and Cherubini 2007: 475) This was a possibility precluded from Hegelianism, which interpreted reality through a dialectic of endless contrasts.

Capitini's early works evinced a certain tendency towards existentialism, marked by his impassioned consciousness of human finitude, which he speaks of in *Elementi di un'esperienza religiosa* (Elements of a religious experience), published in 1937. However, we must not neglect the influence on him of the works of Carlo Michelstaedter, a student from Gorizia who committed suicide in 1910 and who was one of the first to fight for the right of conscientious objection. Capitini was familiar with his works, from which he drew one of the most important terms of his religious philosophy: "persuasion."

Capitini also believed in a "prophetic attitude" by which prophets – unlike priests, who are guardians of dogma and conservatism – push towards the future and innovate by manifesting a subversive, liberating behavior that rejects conservatism. This prophetic attitude was subordinated to "religious persuasion," a term he used to signify faith or belief (Capitini 1950: 57):

> The persuaded one is to prophetic religion what the believer is to traditional religion. But the persuaded one is something more than the believer, because his religious attitude is active, not passive, and the prophetic moment is not external but internal to him: the persuaded one helps keep prophetic tension alive.

> (Bobbio 2011: 33)

This idea of persuasion was rooted in the rejection of social reality and the attempt to transform it. And only through rejection of reality is it possible to work for social change. Religion plays a fundamental role in "transmutation" because it not only transforms social and political reality but acts on a plane that is outside of reality. "Transmutation" is therefore a religious act, and not just an ethical one, characterized by the communion of citizens who together produce the values that characterize *addition*.

All this bears upon his idea of "open religion," in which God is conceived as the God of love and tolerance, but also as the "One-all," an intimate and close God who is the whole of all the subjects committed to creating values that transform reality, to freeing it, so that the needs of all may be heard. Capitini's religiosity does not envision a God outside of reality, and although transcendent, this God lives in the present, accompanying mankind towards its perfection. This explains why Capitini's religion is both spiritual and social.

On these bases Capitini established a topic that encompassed all his prior discourse: "co-presence," namely the presence of all to create the values necessary for transforming reality. It is a union of the living and the dead, an increment in the improvement of reality, an *addition* projected onto the future but also a "dutiful openness to values, beauty, goodness, justice, honesty, purity, the law of good that speaks to us and commands and inspires – if we open ourselves to it – at all times, and raises our individuality, which tends to remain closed, deaf, restless: sin, at bottom, is narrow-mindedness" (Capitini 1955: 9).

This open religion professed by Capitini could not fail to be open to discussion with both Christianity and communism. Indeed, he rejected neither the one nor the other, and did not embrace them either, but accepted them. An acceptance made of *addition* and *transmutation*, which leads to the construction of a new politico-religious reality. A post-communism and a post-Christianity that are not only consequent, but above all reformed. They inhabit a completely new phase, totally different from the previous one.

Regarding the problem of the state, Capitini, like Weil, strongly criticized the fascist idolatry that considered the state to be the pre-eminent institution: a Leviathan that claimed to exercise its power from above through physical coercion and spiritual enslavement. As God was to belong to all, for Capitini so also the state was to belong to all, according to the logic of a correspondence between religious co-presence and political omnicracy, in which this was the answer to the problems that democracy had failed to solve: a goal that can only be reached through a second correspondence, between "open religion" and "open revolution," i.e. a revolution provoked by the *persuaded* through the tools of *noncooperation, nonfalsehood* and *nonviolence*.

Specifically, nonviolence was an indispensable tool for realizing the politico-religious project of Capitini's "co-presence." This was a positive value and therefore, even in writing the word that corresponded to it, the negative meaning produced by writing *non* separately from *violence* needed to be modified by joining the two terms into one word: *non-violence*. This meant not only abandoning violence but also adopting a set of values and techniques by which the rejection of violence was enacted in everyday life.

Like Gandhi, Khan and Weil, Capitini too recognized the importance of the link between means and ends, by which "the purpose of love can only be fulfilled through love, the purpose of honesty by honest means, the purpose of peace not through the old law of such unstable results as 'If you want peace, prepare for war,' but through another law: 'During peace, prepare for peace'" (Capitini 2009: 13). The primacy of action is therefore also crucial in Capitini's vision of nonviolence as a practical commitment, creativity, constructiveness: an open method, in continuous improvement through assiduous additions and continuous experimentation. But in order to perform nonviolent action there is a need for the courage not to destroy one's adversary but to fight him with love and respect, always bearing in mind, as Gandhi said, that we fight sin, not sinners.

Like Gandhi and Weil, Capitini too considered the concept of truth to be a good in itself, a moral law that led to the just, a principle that must be laid at the foundation of *satyagraha* (a term of Gandhi's that he did not hesitate to make his own), since for him too Truth was God, and it was also

> [...] what is truly Value in itself, Good in itself and at the same time the moral Law is what is Just and must be fulfilled; it is the moral order of the world, at the same time the Law and the Lawmaker; it is the moral and divine reality that is beyond the appearances of way; it is at the same time omnipresent and invisible.
>
> (Capitini 2009: 22–23)

Here then Truth and nonviolence were presented as two aspects so interdependent as to be inseparable, because "nonviolence" did not just mean not committing violent actions, but was an all-encompassing lifestyle that even eliminated from one's head wicked thoughts, lies, hatred and contempt.

*Suffering* was another fundamental characteristic of *satyagraha*, closely interconnected with Truth and nonviolence. Indeed, *satyagrahi* required courage precisely to put into practice one's willingness to suffer as a way of persuading one's adversary without subduing him, but by showing him the force and justness of one's convictions.

Together with this vision, profoundly influenced by the Indian independencist experience, was that of the "Muslim Catholic" – as described by Pius XI – Louis Massignon, who interpreted *satyagraha* as a "civic requirement of Truth," which saw *satyagraha* as a civic commitment favoring the social change of reality (Capitini 2009: 25). Nonviolence was therefore a permanent revolution that did not signify radical change as in the case of violent revolutions, but a continuous, incessant change.

Nonviolence was cooperation, the rediscovery of a relationship with God, harmony, flourishing, union, future-tending endeavor, moral choice, co-presence of the living and the dead in an infinite unity that produced collective values progressively transforming history, but also cooperative-tending omnicracy, with grass-roots power exercised more and more collectively. The original element in this description lay in an eagerness to transform reality through nonviolent action, to educate people to an omnicratic participation in the exercise of power, in an effort to bring about social change aimed at listening and the co-presence of the One-all: the individual within the wholeness of reality.

## The institutional pacifism of Norberto Bobbio

With our focus still on Italian and European pacifism in the period between the world wars and the post-war period, we cannot overlook Norberto Bobbio's important contribution, especially from the second half of the 1960s onwards, when what he himself called "institutional pacifism" began to take shape.

Bobbio's reflections on the subjects of peace and nonviolence were largely inspired by Cold War anxieties and by the questions that people in general and philosophers in particular were duty-bound to pose in the presence of thermonuclear weapons capable of annihilating all of humanity. So, unlike Capitini, who had approached the topics of nonviolence and civil resistance during the fascist period, Bobbio – who knew the work of Capitini and held its elements of originality in high esteem – began a serious study of peace only later on.

It was during the fascist period that "Aldo [Capitini] had become a reference point for a serious and severe ethico-religious opposition, from which the clandestine movement of liberal socialism took shape, through his friendship with Calogero, and became one of the future components of the Action Party" (Bobbio 2004: 42). Bobbio also took part in the meetings of this group, and the experience marked his transition from the passive resistance conditioned by the well-known philo-fascism of his family to an active resistance.

The new doctrine of liberal socialism was the first anti-fascist cultural movement of non-Marxist inspiration to break off from the tradition of Benedetto Croce (which had had a great but paralysing influence) by embodying an ideologico-political platform that responded to the most vital needs of young intellectuals (Zangrandi 1964: 193–94). It was precisely these features that enabled the group to carry on an active resistance of proselytization by pasting up handwritten flyers or strips of paper with pacifist slogans. The attempt was also made to maintain relations with the armed partisan groups, even though they themselves never took up arms.

It should also be noted that the Resistance period in Italy and the rest of Europe was substantially characterized by three different forms of opposition to Nazi fascism: active, armed and passive:

> Armed resistance was part of active resistance. But there was an active resistance that was unarmed. It consisted of those who made false documents and identity cards, or those who turned out propaganda. They also took risks. If they had the bad luck to get arrested they'd end up in concentration camps too. The gray area, which today has been pardoned, were the so-called fence-sitters, who waited to see which way the wind was blowing. They were people who didn't want to get into trouble. None of them actually rooted for the Germans, but they played it safe.
>
> (Bobbio 2004: 73)

Participation in the Resistance led Bobbio to political commitment by joining the Action Party, which confirmed his predisposition to being a contemplative individual rather than active.

For someone like him who had come of age under a totalitarian regime, once fascism had been defeated and the war had ended, it was imperative to try to eliminate the problems that hindered democracy and national and international peace. The only way this could be accomplished was to eliminate violence as a means of resolving international disputes, as the United Nations proposed to do in its Charter, adopted on 26 June 1945 in San Francisco.

Much of Bobbio's writings on peace and pacifism are contained in two collections: *Il problema della guerra e le vie della pace* (The problem of war and the pathways of peace), published in 1979, and *Il terzo assente* (The absent third) of 1989. But he also argued his position on war and in particular on just war in the news media, especially *La Stampa* of Turin, a newspaper Bobbio collaborated with from 1976 on.

In general, Bobbio's pacifism went through two phases: the first from the 1960s and the second from the 1990s, in particular from the first Gulf War of 1991. As Bobbio himself reported in his *Autobiografia* (Autobiography) published in 1997, his thoughts on the danger of nuclear war and nuclear awareness arose when Einaudi asked him to write a preface for the Italian edition of *Hiroshima Is Everywhere: Diary from Hiroshima and Nagasaki* (1961) by Günther Anders, who was also the author of *Burning Conscience: The Case of the Hiroshima Pilot Claude Eatherly, Told in His Letters to Günther Anders* (1962). Bobbio was especially fascinated by Anders' idea of proposing

> a moral code, which – faced with the threat of mankind's annihilation – would enunciate new duties binding on all human beings. His vision was directed to the moral transformation of humanity and imposed an absolute prohibition on the use of atomic weapons. Anders was quite clear about opposing institutional pacifism to moral pacifism. He believed that new institutions could only be effective on the foundation of a new morality.
>
> (Bobbio 2004: 221–22)

However, Bobbio, who did not believe a new moral code could be created, took the other path, that of *institutional pacifism*.

Despite this choice, he remained equally sensitive to issues on the moral conduct of people in war, expressing, for example, the firm conviction that, faced with the threat of nuclear war, it was everyone's duty to be conscientious objectors.

> Conscientious objection means refusal to bear arms. When in the category of arms we include a bomb that alone has the explosive power of half of all the bombs dropped in the last war, I wonder if bearing arms hasn't become a problem of conscience not only for objectors protesting in the name of their religious faith, but for each of us, in the name of humanity. Conscientious objection literally refers to a situation in which the imperative of conscience forbids us to commit injustice. If we ask our conscience, we can no longer refuse to recognize that today we are all, at least potentially, objectors.
>
> (Bobbio 1989: 129–42)

The first essay contained in the collection *Il problema della guerra* was written in 1966 and is entitled "Il problema della guerra e le vie della pace" (The problem of war and the pathways of peace"). Being its most complete contribution on the subject, it gave its title to the entire work. It began with three possible interpretive metaphors of history: the fly in the bottle, the fish in the net, or the labyrinth. The metaphor of the fly in the bottle recalled a famous saying of Wittgenstein's that the task of philosophy was to teach a fly to get out of a bottle; this meant that there was a way out (image of the open bottle) and that there was someone outside of the bottle (the philosopher) who knew the way out. The saying about the fish in the net was different because in this case there was no way out: the fish was writhing and flapping to get out, but it didn't know it couldn't do so until the net had been opened, and at that point it wouldn't be to get free but to perish. Both of the previous metaphors presuppose the action of a superior entity that resolves the situation of constraint, and for this reason, in Bobbio's opinion, only the third image, that of the labyrinth, is able to fully portray the human condition. The individual believes they know that there is a way out but that they don't know where it is. Since there is no one except themselves to show it to them, they must seek it alone (Bobbio 2004: 226). It was a journey made up of dead ends, streets that led nowhere but whose purpose was to show the impassable limits beyond which no one could or should go. One of these dead ends was thermonuclear war, a path that was no longer viable because it could annihilate the whole of humanity.

Yet this idea of reality as a labyrinth presupposes a Hegelian conception of history not only as a process, but above all as a becoming, as progress. This is certainly a rational choice that Bobbio makes, but with "the attitude of one who flees from nostalgia for the past, rejects the great impossible recurrences, doesn't try to turn back, as we often say, the clock of history" (Bobbio: 1997: 36).

As he himself clarified in *Il problema della guerra*, to say that war is a dead end meant essentially two things:

(a) war is an outworn institution that has had its day and is destined to disappear; (b) war is an unseemly or unjust or impious institution that must be eliminated. In other words, the end of war is now a foregone conclusion, but what remains to be seen is whether this event is a human prediction or a project.

(Bobbio 1997: 37)

The conclusions he arrived at led to two respective pacifist attitudes: *passive pacifism* or *active pacifism*. The first approach regarded war as such a catastrophic event that it had to be considered an unusable instrument destined to disappear over time; the second approach considered war as a danger with consequences so apocalyptic and contrary to commonly shared human values that every effort must be made to eliminate it. And if the watch-and-wait attitude (typical of realists) corresponded to the balance of terror according to which peace was entrusted not to a historic balance of power but to the new condition of a balance of powerlessness, the other, active one (typical of idealists) was to strive to raise an atomic consciousness, so as "to realize that peace is not a process but a conquest (as all conquests can also be, once conquered, lost)" (Bobbio 1997: 56).

Based on the above reasoning, Bobbio naturally emphasized the importance of active pacifism in order to make his readers aware of the fact that
thermonuclear war could not be considered to be on an equal footing with
wars of the past, for at least three reasons:

1  What he defined as a "philosophical" or "metaphysical" reason, in the
   fact that never before in history had war jeopardized the survival of all
   of humanity.
2  An equally philosophical realization that all the theories historically
   adopted to justify or support war were no longer applicable to nuclear war.
3  A utilitarian awareness that

> Thermonuclear war serves no purpose. The first aim of war is victory
> [...]. But as the potency of weapons increases it will become increas-
> ingly difficult, in the event war breaks out in all its horror, to distinguish
> the winner from the loser: the only winners might be the non-belli-
> gerents, the neutrals, or more simply those fortuitously spared from the
> carnage.
>
> (Bobbio 1997: 42)

It was no longer possible to say that war was useful for the moral progress
of society, as Humboldt, Hegel or Nietzsche did, nor for civic progress, as it
was for Cattaneo and Cousin, nor for technological progress, because the
study of defensive and offensive weapons risked destroying the entire human
race. In these terms, war took on the aspect of an irrational, insane and
destructive phenomenon devoid of any moral or rational justification.

> For him not only has it become untenable to maintain that war is a
> factor of progress but also that technical and scientific progress may
> lead to a gradual containment of war. In reality, the balance of nuclear
> terror does not aim at the gradual phasing out of war, but lives on
> precisely from the permanent possibility of war, a possibility that it
> constantly encourages through technico-scientific research and the
> production of ever more sophisticated and destructive weapons.
>
> (Zolo 2008: 86–87)

As a result, during the period in which he wrote *Il problema della guerra*,
and up to the outbreak of the 1991 Gulf War, Bobbio was also critical of the
*bellum justum* (the just war), a theory he felt was used alternately to deny the
validity of warmonger and pacifist theories and that justified war as an
attempt to remedy a suffered wrong. The basic problem, however, was that

any war could be considered right by both parties and therefore determined no legally definitive situation but a tangle to unravel. Moreover, if the aim of a just war was that the right side should win, the conclusion turned out to be the opposite, since in any case it sustained the winner.

Not even the moral legitimacy of the defensive war of a state attacked by another state made sense in the nuclear age. Since the distinction between offensive and defensive war got blurred, thermonuclear conflict became a return to the state of Hobbesian nature, the antithesis of the rule of law that mankind had struggled to build by means of law.

In line with this reasoning, in the preface to the first edition of *Il problema della guerra*, Norberto Bobbio wrote:

> I don't consider myself a militant nonviolent, but I've acquired the absolute certainty that people will succeed in resolving their conflicts without resorting to violence, in particular that collective and organized violence which is war, both external and internal, or else violence will annihilate them from the face of the earth. The importance of the movements that preach collective and active nonviolence derives from the increased awareness that as violence becomes more complete it becomes even more ineffective.
>
> (Bobbio 1997: 26–27)

His was an active pacifism that might have taken more than one path: that of *ethical pacifism*, that of *instrumental pacifism* or as it later did that of *institutional pacifism*.

While ethical pacifism followed the Gandhian tradition, and in Italy, also Capitini's religious pacifism, which distinguished passive and active nonviolence by the ethical means of conducting conflicts, instrumental pacifism contained within itself theories that favored peace through disarmament but with the scruple that the state which first decided to limit its armaments would be more vulnerable than others; and institutional or juridical pacifism – Bobbio's chosen solution – was based on the idea that a superstate or a world state needed to be established. Bobbio was firmly convinced that what made the use of violence indispensable, when a crucial stage of international friction was reached, was the lack of an authority that superseded those of individual states, capable of limiting their discretionary power and establishing which party was wrong or right. That authority could be none other than a single, universal state superseding all other states that made up the international community:

> In light of such considerations, Bobbio sketched out his original way to peace, to which he gave the name "juridical pacifism." Bobbio

believed that a more peaceful world order could only result from new international institutions that went beyond the system of sovereign states and gave powers of politico-military intervention to a supranational authority. In his view, this was the threshold of rationality that humanity had to pass to renounce the risk of self-destruction. From this perspective, Bobbio maintained that the United Nations represented a foreshadowing and almost the nucleus of those "central institutions" that in future would be capable of guaranteeing the conditions of a stable and universal peace.

(Bellamy *et al.* 2004: 80)

This was a solution that did not purport to totally eliminate the use of violence, but at least to effectively regulate and limit it by going beyond the "Westphalia system" in favor of a strong central authority identifiable in the United Nations.

It was a pacifism that had its roots in law and was clearly influenced by Hobbes' and Kant's thought, reinterpreting Hobbes' natural law precept in a Kantian sense, by "giving it a universalist and cosmopolitan value," and interpreting Kant in Hobbesian terms by "assigning to Kant's federalism the meaning of an authentic project for overcoming the sovereignty of nation states and establishing a 'world state'" (Zolo 2008: 90).

From Hobbes Bobbio had imported not only the idea of contractualism, but also the two categories that characterized it (the *pactum societatis* and of the *pactum subjectionis*), considering that to move from a situation of international anarchy to an orderly and peaceful political system it was necessary for states to subscribe both to a *pactum societatis* and a *pactum subjectionis*, that is to say to agree to confer on a "third," *super partes* authority the power to regulate their relations and possible disputes.

And from Kant's *Perpetual Peace* Bobbio took the principle that nation states which wanted to join the *world state* should all have the common feature of being republics. That is, if not true democracies, at least constitutional states that recognized citizens' rights:

This, according to Bobbio, is the condition for keeping the power of the international Leviathan from being oppressive and for making the international system more of an "international democracy" capable of protecting human rights beyond the borders of individual states as well as against their claim to absolute sovereignty. Peace and democracy imply each other, while despotism can be considered the continuation of war within the state.

(Zolo 2008: 91–92)

So, according to Bobbio's interpretation, the establishment of the United Nations meant the international community had definitively embarked on the path that led to legal/institutional pacifism, but this lacked an essential characteristic: despite the fact that the United Nations was the result of a *pactum societatis*, it was devoid of a *pactum subjectionis*, that is, the subordination of states to a common power that held exclusive sway over the exercise of coercion. The United Nations, despite having taken a step forward from the previous League of Nations – which was a mere association of states – had failed to give rise to a superstate, an institution that enjoyed sovereign power and a legitimate monopoly of force. Nonetheless, an important goal was reached: Articles 42 and 43 of the Charter gave it the power to take military action when this became necessary to restore peace. Bobbio, however, was convinced that the process of superstate democratization would remain incomplete as long as the principle of supranational sovereignty came into conflict with that of state sovereignty.

It was these theoretico-political premises that gave rise to what may be considered the second phase of Bobbio's pacifism. The event that determined a more tolerant position on conflicts was the outbreak of the Gulf War on 17 January 1991. Interviewed by Antonio Leone for Rai's *Tg3* on 15 January 1991, Bobbio argued that the war that was about to take place could be considered a just war for two reasons:

1   it was founded on international law, having received the United Nations' go-ahead as an action aimed at self-defense;
2   its effectiveness depended on certain conditions: it would be so if it were successful, rapid and limited to the area affected by the conflict.

He held that the war was just, not because he had suddenly begun to appreciate the justificationist theories he had previously rejected in the 1960s, but because the conflict was in conformity with law, "legal." "Having witnessed an aggression against a sovereign state and thus a blatant violation of international law, the United Nations had a duty to react to the aggression by resorting in turn to the use of military force" (Zolo 2008: 95). And even if it was true that the force was not directly employed by the Security Council, as prescribed by Chapter 12 of the Charter, what represented for him a substantial change was the decision not to entrust the resolution of the dispute to the traditional right of self-defense, but to an entity superior to the individual states.

The intransigence of his rejection of any kind of conflict, which he had manifested since the threat of thermonuclear apocalypse, was now tempered but was never categorically called into question. The test of his consistency would be the debate that arose concerning the matter and the voices of those strongly critical of his opinion, which to a great many appeared to directly contradict his previous profession of faith in pacifism. Among the first people to take a position were Massimo Cacciari and Cesare Luporini. Cacciari referred to the old historical meanings of "just" as a characterization of purposes usually of religious content, comparing the concept of a just war to that of *jihad* and wondering if, to date, in a secular civilization,

> does it make sense to speak of "just war" outside of perspectives of value? Does it make sense to speak of "just war" where the expression "justice" does not correspond to factual assessments? Indeed, what do we mean today by "just war"? Only the answer to the naked *fact* of an aggression. But it is patently absurd and illogical to establish any criterion of "justice" on facts.
>
> (Cacciari 1991: 19)

If in the Western world a politics with religious justifications could be comparable to idolatry, the only way to justify a war as "just" would be to refer to its causes, namely to have Western political forms prevail over Eastern ones in an attempt to impose this model of democracy.

Luporini, in agreement with Cacciari, considered absolutely short-sighted those who, beyond the short-term consequences, did not take into account the long-term ones that might intensify international terrorism and cultural misunderstandings. In this regard, the Gulf War risked inadvertently supporting the ideology of "religious war" whose aim would be to foment rebellions against an oppressive, predatory West (Luporini 1991: 14).

In addition to Cacciari and Luporini, fifty other Turinese intellectuals – many of them ex-students of Bobbio's – took a stand against him and in an open letter, published in *Il Manifesto* under the title "Gli intellettuali non possono tacere" (Intellectuals cannot be silent), argued that a war could never be a fair or effective tool for resolving disputes because of the environmental, social and political effects it would create.

The dispute did not leave Bobbio unperturbed. Pained by the participation of Arnaldo Bagnasco, Guido Neppi Modona, Gianni Vattimo, Gian Mario Bravo, Angelo Tartaglia, Gian Giangiacomo Migone and Gastone Cotino, he insisted that the case in point was to be considered an example of a *just war*:

> I have repeatedly affirmed that in the face of nuclear war it is probably no longer possible to distinguish between just wars and unjust wars, because it is no longer possible to distinguish a war of defense from a war of offense. But in conventional warfare the distinction is

still possible, and in the case of Iraq's invasion of Kuwait, it is certain and continues to exist. Moreover, the United Nations Charter itself, whose original main purpose was to ensure a stable peace, recognizes the legitimacy of a war of self-defense, and in some of its basic articles even establishes the formation of armed forces (armed!) to take urgent military measures to re-establish international order.

(Bobbio 1991a: 7)

In this case, therefore, the war could only be just, but, he asked his critics, for the most part inspired by the ideals of the Resistance, if at this point they considered that even the war of liberation was unjust.

The answers were not long in coming. Tartaglia, a professor at the Polytechnic University, stated that the purpose of the letter sent to *Il Manifesto* was not to challenge Bobbio, but to reiterate that all wars were unjust because they had never solved any problems, because the stronger was not always in the right and because present wars always laid the basis for future ones. As far as the Resistance was concerned, he pointed out that this had a different character because revolt against a tyrant, as defined by Thomas Aquinas, was always permitted.

Gian Marco Bravo too insisted that no war was just, not even the Resistance, but that should be considered a misleading comparison, because it was like defending yourself from someone who punches you (Angelico and De Gennaro 1991: iii).

Even Mario Bin, a professor of law, maintained in regard to the Resistance that Bobbio had fallen into error, while Giacomo Migone acknowledged Bobbio's honesty and intellectual courage:

because it takes a lot of courage to disagree with the powerful, and Bobbio does so, but it takes even more courage to disagree with friends. Anyway, Bobbio will agree that the application of the principle of legality is decisive for the purpose of its realization. Bobbio himself says that the ultimatum given to Saddam made negotiation more difficult.

(Angelico and De Gennaro 1991: iii)

A position in sharp contrast with Bobbio's was also taken by Danilo Zolo, professor of philosophy of international law, who in an article entitled "Che differenza c'è tra la 'guerra giusta' e 'Allah Akbar'" (What is the difference between a "just war" and "Allah Akbar") wrote:

I think Bobbio is wrong, and it is a painful surprise for me to realize I am in serious disagreement with him. It amazes me first of all that in the midst of the nuclear age he resorts to a category, the "just war," which I thought was by now confined to those manuals of moral theology which for centuries offered excellent arguments to all the parties involved to justify religious wars or to justify any kind of war as a war of religion.

(Zolo 1991: 13)

For Zolo, proclaiming within the Western world that the war against Iraq was just corresponded to crying "Allah Akbar," "God is with us," "the right is on our side," thus justifying a "(secular) holy war." The United Nations was very far – still in Zolo's opinion – from being a morally and juridically correct international body, first because in the past it had committed serious errors that had worsened the Palestinian situation, and second because in many cases the United Nations had been unable or unwilling to respond to violations of international law by the superpowers, to the detriment of the minor ones.

In answer to all the criticisms that had rained down on him, on 22 January 1991 Bobbio published an article in *L'Unità* entitled "Ci sono ancora guerre giuste? Me lo chiedo" (Are there still just wars? I wonder). Contrary to his opponents, he continued to believe that just war was neither obsolete nor a historical relic nor a concept confined to the manuals of moral theology. Nor was "just war = holy war" an appropriate equation:

Just war failed because in a legal system such as the international one in which there was no independent judge above the parties, each of the two contenders put forward arguments to support the justness of its cause and wars always ended up being just on both sides. But contrary to what my critics seem to believe, the effect of abandoning the doctrine of just war was not the principle "all wars are unjust"; but exactly the opposite principle: "all wars are just." The "*jus ad bellum*," that is the right to make war, was considered a prerogative of sovereign power.

(Bobbio 1991b: 1)

The distinction between lawful and unlawful use of force, on which every justification of just war was based, had once again become relevant thanks to the San Francisco Conference, which initiated the UN Charter, which regulated wars of self-defense, international sanctions and the employment of international armed force. However, the rejection of war as categorically unjust could not preclude the possibility of distinguishing victim from aggressor; rather, this marked an obligatory phase, before the outbreak of a war, in which all attempts at peaceful solution of a dispute should be undertaken:

I confess that after these recent days I too am far from tranquil. But would we have been any more tranquil in the opposite case? It is hard today to give an answer because we can't yet predict if the necessary conditions for the use of force will be satisfied [...] the lesser evil: that it be circumscribed in area and limited in time. But one point must remain firm: renouncing force in certain cases doesn't mean eliminating force from the game but only favoring the force of the bully.

(Bobbio 1991b: 1)

The debate arising from the outbreak of the Gulf War continued along these lines throughout 1991.

In 1992 Domenico Losurdo once again questioned Norberto Bobbio on his position in the light of the press reports about heinous crimes, massacres of those in flight, bombings of water networks, etc., carried out in order to severely punish Saddam Hussein and keep the price of oil low by avoiding an oil crisis that would slow down the economic expansionism of the West. Despite such shocking reports, Bobbio had no second thoughts, as he believed that at that time it was necessary to block Saddam's expansionist ambitions, which flagrantly challenged the international order.

Despite his interventionism, Bobbio never failed to express his doubts about the effectiveness of war as a means of resolving conflicts. In view of the grief, destruction and risks of escalation that the long-standing conflict was carrying in its wake, he eventually took a contrary position, which he communicated in an article published in *La Stampa* entitled "Questa volta dico no" (This time I say no). In it he expressed all his dismay both with the methods used by the United States and the repeated bombings of Baghdad:

Hateful and unworthy of a civilized nation, thoroughly unworthy of the greatest power on earth, which is also a great democracy, and as such should be an example to other peoples of prudence, common sense, wisdom, respect for the law, and basic moral principles, like that of refraining from slaughter unless in extreme cases of self-defense or a state of necessity. I don't see any of these decent qualities in the bombings. On the contrary, it amazes me that, apart from certain noble exceptions, such as that of the newspaper I write for, Scardocchia's article from the United States or Gorbachev's stern warning, the reaction of public opposition has been rather weak and, even worse, there has been an almost unanimous acquiescence of Western governments, which can only be deemed vile and servile.

(Bobbio 1993: 1–2)

## The nonviolent means for social change in the sociology of Danilo Dolci

The last person we will examine in this chapter is Danilo Dolci, a socio-political activist, sociologist and nonviolent Italian who from the 1950s until the day of his death dedicated his life to fighting the Mafia and violence in all its manifestations, by promoting new forms of socio-economic development in poverty-stricken places.

His efforts at social reform developed throughout twentieth-century Italy and were certainly affected by the economic boom of the 1960s (which helped to improve living conditions), the culture of dissent of the 1960s–1970s (which demanded a new openness to progressive change), and the advent of television and mass communication (Vigilante 2012: 14).

Dolci was born in 1924 in Sesana in the province of Trieste (today Slovenia) of an Italian-German father employed in the state railway and a Slovenian mother. He studied architecture, first in Milan and later in Rome, where he fled in 1943 to avoid the call to arms of the Republic of Salò. After the war, Danilo returned to live with his parents in Pozzolo Formigaro, near Alessandria, and re-enrolled in the University of Milan without ever completing his degree.

In 1948, Danilo met Father David Maria Turoldo, who spoke to him for the first time of the community led by Don Zeno Saltini, called Noma-delfia ("brotherhood is law"), an experiment inspired by the Catholic and socialist ferments of the 1930s:

> In 1950 he abandoned his studies and went to Fossoli, a hamlet of Carpi in the province of Modena, to join the "Piccoli Apostoli" community founded in 1946 by Don Zeno Saltini in the former Nazi concentration camp, under the name of Nomadelfia ("brotherhood is law"). He remained there for just over a year, as Saltini's secretary, working with an authentic evangelical spirit even at the humblest jobs, to help the marginalized and war orphans.
>
> (Ragone 2011: 14)

The experience enabled Dolci to obtain his first insights into the weight attributed to the phase of individual awareness of one's basic needs, abilities and interests, an awareness that came to fruition in the community experience, where needs, skills and interests are added up in a group context to achieve common goals more easily and effectively than at the individual level.

While maintaining his involvement in the Nomadelfia experiment, in 1952 Danilo left the community, which had become his refuge, and returned home, where he stayed briefly before leaving for Trappeto, a small town in Sicily he had lived in with his family from 1941 to 1942 when his father's railway job had brought him there. Now he was returning with thirty *lire* [2] and a great desire to help the people of Trappeto, one of the poorest towns in Sicily:

> What he discovered in Trappeto was massive unemployment leading to large-scale emigration and banditry, malnutrition, primitive living conditions (the sewage systems consisted of an open ditch running through the middle of the village), and a general sense of fatalism and hopelessness. While Dolci quickly understood that the main problem was lack of jobs, he also realized that underlying the economic issues was *omertà*, the Sicilian code of silence that compelled people to keep to themselves and trust no one outside the immediate family. The result of centuries of foreign exploitation and, more recently, Mafia intimidation and violence, *omertà* rendered social and economic development even more problematic.
>
> (Baldassaro 2015: 100–1)

With the help of some of his Nomadelfia friends and savings from manual labor jobs he purchased two hectares of land just outside the village, in Serro, to build his Borgo di Dio (Village of God). There, with the help of local peasants and fishermen, he built a road to the village and a small house to accommodate himself and the orphans who lived in the old section of Trappeto. The town suffered from chronic underdevelopment and incapacity to change because of the widespread banditry that was especially rife between Partinico and Montelepre.

The death of Benedetto Barretta – one of the orphans – from malnutrition in 1952 deeply affected Dolci. After contacting the local and regional authorities to request funding to meet the town's basic needs, he began his first hunger strike, lying symbolically in the same bed where Barretta had died (Baldassaro 2015: 101). His fast lasted eight days and was interrupted only when he had also obtained funds to cover the open sewers. In those eight long days there were demonstrations of sympathy and solidarity from all over Italy, even from Aldo Capitini, with whom he later kept up a lively correspondence which inspired his projects and philosophy of nonviolence.

After his nonviolent protest Dolci undertook the systematic job of gathering data and reporting the results describing the terrible living conditions of the local population. His technique of data collection was to meticulously describe, denounce and reflect on the town's economic and social conditions, and to do interviews outlining the degradation in which the interviewees lived. The result of this work was "Fare presto (e bene) perché si muore," published in 1954 (translated into English as "To Feed the Hungry"):

You get me: I'm not saying we shouldn't pray, meditate, etc. etc. What I'm saying is that in this area [...] people are dying of hunger and many survive because they make do working in the fields of others. And I want to inject the well-founded suspicion that some are dying because of our indifference and neglect.

(Dolci 1954: 101)

The strike and the book of denunciation earned Dolci a certain notoriety that enabled him to initiate a dialogue with the local political world – especially with members of the Communist Party – and the public institutions of Partinico.

In 1955 Laterza published *Banditi a Partinico* ("The outlaws of Partinico") with a preface by Norberto Bobbio. It was Dolci's new book-length denunciation of the injustice in Partinico that for the first time addressed the topic of banditry. The text had a three-part structure, each with a different approach to the subject. The first part was essentially a statistical and environmental description of the area and its population; the second was a series of interviews with the area's inhabitants, including the bandits themselves; and the third was the personal diary Dolci kept during his research:

In the main area of Sicilian banditry (Partinico, Trappeto, Montelepre: 33,000 inhabitants), of the 350 "outlaws," only one has both parents who attended the fourth grade of elementary school. A total of about 650 years of schooling (on average not even the second grade, and what a second grade!) compares to 3,000 years of prison. And the trials against "the bandits" continue. Over a 100 are mentally ill, crippled and deaf and dumb. Each month we spend 13 million lire on police, "law enforcement," jail. More than 150 million a year, while, for example, from the twenty-eight social assistance schools now operating in Italy not one person has graduated. Four thousand people need immediate employment. Inefficiency, the disorder of public life persists. In nine years we've intervened by spending more than 2.5 billion lire of public money to kill and jail while we haven't moved a finger, for example, to use the water of the nearby river (meanwhile more than 40 billion lire has been wasted elsewhere); and this would have easily given work to everyone. If there had been work, there wouldn't have been any banditry.

(Dolci 2009: 27–28)

Dolci chose to talk about banditry instead of the Mafia because in this context it gave a more immediate picture of the Sicilian question (Ragone 2011: 18). Poverty, ignorance, resignation to one's destiny, and violence were the fertile ground where banditry had struck its roots. Yet this degradation, backwardness and despair were due to the void left by the public institutions, which, unable to instruct, educate and train, relied on police and military methods to maintain law and order. The means by which the state acted in these areas prevented it from getting to the heart of the problem, which was entirely social and economic.

On 27 November 1955, Danilo began his second fast at Spine Sante (Partinico). His goal was to get the government's approval to build a dam on the Jato River to collect the winter waters. The project would enable the farmers to irrigate their fields without pandering to the Mafia organization that until then had rationed the water. The dam had been identified as an indispensable factor for economic and social change in the area ever since the first meetings devoted to grass-roots self-analysis, whose purpose was to clarify the truly essential needs and interests of the population (Ragone 2011: 18).

On 30 January 1956, Dolci started his "fast of a thousand," a mass fasting in which farmers and fishermen participated on the San Cataldo beach in Trappeto to protest against the illegal fishing by the Mafia that sharply curtailed the livelihood of the local fishing community. To then fight the problem of unemployment in Partinico and its vicinity, Dolci decided to set up a "reverse strike" to redevelop an unusable road abandoned by local administrators.

> His plan was to lead a group of unemployed men to refurbish a public road that was in disrepair. On 2 February 1956, after widely publicizing the planned protest, even on national television, Dolci, together with about 200 men, began to rebuild the road. Within an hour several truckloads of police arrived. When Dolci refused an order to stop the work, he and six others were arrested and taken to the Ucciardone prison in Palermo.
>
> Dolci's arrest became front-page news and generated a debate in the Italian Parliament. The historic trial that followed in April made the 31-year-old activist a *cause célèbre* and gained him the support of prominent European intellectuals such as Jean-Paul Sartre and Carlo Levi. Dolci was acquitted on the more serious charges of sedition and violently resisting arrest but convicted of trespassing and sentenced to fifty days in prison, equal to the time he had already served.
>
> (Baldassaro 2015: 102)

In 1958 Danilo Dolci was awarded the Lenin Peace Prize for his work in favor of the peace of peoples. Dolci accepted the award, stressing how it was the result of a nonviolent pursuit of the pathways for peace and the grass-roots activism of civil society. On that occasion he also explained that he would use the prize money to found a local Center for Studies and Initiatives for Full Employment. It was the first discussion ever held in Italy on the topic of full employment.

Dolci founded the first such Center in Partinico in May of that same year, and it was soon followed by other offices in Roccamena, Corleone, Menfi, Cammarata, and San Giovanni Gemini. The Centers undertook to train and educate local elites and managers to perform the task of changing Sicilian society from within. As Ragone points out (2011: 25), the Centers for Full Employment were very similar to Aldo Capitini's COS (the Social Orientation Centers) and Guido Calogero's Centers for the Professional Education in Social Assistance.

What more than anything characterized Dolci's work up to then, and what would continue to characterize it in the future, was his "maieutic" method:

> Everyone has ideas and convictions, which may be the result of personal reflection, or the sediment of a tradition never subjected to the scrutiny of reason, or the result of a conditioning by those who have the tools to direct public opinion. Discussing your beliefs in groups enables you to pass them through a sieve to separate the wheat from the chaff. In this sense groups have a maieutic function: everyone helps others to verify, deepen and understand better. It's important to note that the setting – chairs in a circle – is already in itself a negation of any hierarchy in communication. In all maieutic groups, even those who, like children or women, aren't used to expressing themselves (or rather aren't encouraged to do so), the participants have the right and freedom to speak out. It's at the same time extremely simple, natural, and deeply innovative.
>
> (Vigilante 2012: 77)

This was the maieutic method: an instrument to make the poor and socially excluded part of a group discussion that aimed primarily to promote a psycho-social change, through an awareness of their ability to bring change to the surrounding reality, and later also an administrative and local-institutional change.

In order for these types of change to take place, it was essential for Dolci to become aware of people's untapped potential and the structural and cultural factors that prevented change at the local level. Only after gaining an awareness of the conditions that had condemned them to a life of misery could they work together as a community to promote change. It was a question of favoring not only action in the strictly economic sense linked to the alleviation of poverty, but also and above all a process of popular self-analysis that helped people in these places to become aware of the unacceptability of the situation they were in and the need to take action to change it (Vigilante 2012: 113).

An example of this is the 1960 Congress on Health Conditions in Palma di Montechiaro (in the area of Agrigento), an underdeveloped area of Sicily (Ragone 2011: 27). A parasitologist from the University of Rome, Dr. Silvio Pampiglione, analyzed the environmental health conditions of the town, and was deeply struck by the fact that all of the approximately 600 families in the study lived in houses of mortar and plaster full of humidity (when they were not dug into the rock from which rainwater often filtered), without running water or bathrooms, and with the stench of the open-air street sewers, and hordes of mice and flies (Deaglio 1993: 130–31). The Congress was the occasion for a scientific analysis of the many reasons for the health problems in this area of Sicily and those like it, from the multiple points of view of doctors, planners, agricultural technicians, sociologists, etc.

On this occasion, Dolci explained the core of his reasoning at that time (which would then become the contents of a book): the "waste" of the potential of men and women forced to live in unhealthy conditions through archaic beliefs, superstitions, prejudices and Mafia violence.

It is a primitive world of witchcraft and evil spells, seers and con-jurors, treasure seekers and the possessed. And Mafiosi. In the area between Cammarata and Palma di Montechiaro, the relationship between the Mafia and the population seems no different from that of tapeworms and the intestines: a situation of parasitism palmed off as mutual adaptation indispensable for well-being. After making excel-lent reports about the relations of the local Mafioso with everyone, including authorities and priests, one of [the town of] Mussomeli's informers concludes: "The Mafia does an important service, not because the population is afraid, but because they're in command [...] because these commanders are all a group, and maintain discipline in the town." These commanders, who made up a single group, were the Mafiosi, the politicians, the priests and the police.

(Vigilante 2012: 114–15)

The event opened the eyes of the community, which for the first time realized that they lived in poverty and had to wake up from the torpor of their fatalism and make a change. Unfortunately, because of the low quality of the public administration and social capital in Sicily as a whole, the people of Palma di Montechiaro were unable to build on their new awareness and the local authorities could not even collect and use the funds made available by the Cassa del Mezzogiorno (a development fund for the South of Italy) once the spotlight was focused on the scandalous conditions of those people's lives.

In 1960 Danilo Dolci also published *Spreco* ("Waste"), an account of his subsequent work in the villages of the Valle del Belice and the Valle del Carboj. Through his usual techniques of interviews and data collection, he highlighted the inverse relationship of waste and economic development. In this investigative book the concept of waste was developed from several viewpoints: from the Mafia murders as a waste of human lives, to the problems of agrarian reform as waste of land, to the lack of public works as a waste of water. All these wastes pointed to the need for the type of change that could be brought about by "democratic planning" that "… start[s] from something more basic … [and] promote[s] clarity and awareness at the grass-roots level" (Dolci 1960: 25).

To broaden his knowledge of planning experiences and to enrich his ideas on democratic planning, Danilo began to take trips abroad. Among his destinations were India, Israel, the United States and the USSR. His travel reports were published in the *Ora* of Palermo, where he had started working as a correspondent. Danilo's incessant information gathering and dissemination of results and knowledge took him on numerous trips around Italy to explain the activity of his Centers for Studies and Initiatives for Full Employment, which deviated from the traditional tools of capitalism and communism, developing a new method for the creation and transformation of social relations.

> The community dimension that Dolci has in mind has thus been summarized by L. Ghersi: it takes place at the level of micro-structures, conceived not as totalizing entities, but as a community in which mutual communication is really possible on an equal basis, so as not to lose any creative contribution that individuals are capable of. Each microstructure is, in itself, a factor of social change, and a place for experimentation with new job opportunities, new economic relationships, new customs, a new mentality. The various microstructures communicate with each other, cooperate and mutually support each other, building a network of experimentation in social and economic relationships as an alternative to the old institutions. As this network spreads and grows with new contributions, we'll finally bring about a change in the ways of building and organizing macrostructures, that is, the larger territorial entities, states, and eventually the entire international community.
>
> (Ragone 2011: 30)

On 29 October 1963, Dolci started a new hunger strike in Roccamena for the construction of the dam on the Belice river to provide local populations with benefits like those produced by the dam on the Jato River. On 7 March 1964, he decided to occupy the main square of Roccamena with 100 villagers and forcibly demand the construction of the Belice dam and the rescinding of the law on emphyteusis (the right to property under a long-term or perpetual lease), which later took place by an Act of the national Parliament. His awareness-raising and anti-Mafia campaigns earned him the hatred of Cardinal Ruffini in Palermo, who accused him of discrediting Sicily and Sicilians by claiming that the public and ecclesiastical institutions were lax and neglectful in managing the area.

In September 1965, upon gathering fifty affidavits – collected in a file entitled "Chi gioca solo" ("He who plays alone")[3] – in a conference at the Rome Press Club, Danilo Dolci and Franco Alasia denounced the widespread collusion and pervasive patronage of the political elite and Mafia of Sicily:

> [...] he and Franco Alasia, his closest collaborator, made a more direct assault when they appeared before the Italian Parliament's Anti-Mafia Commission. Armed with fifty signed affidavits obtained from courageous witnesses, they described the collusion between fourteen notable Sicilian politicians and the Mafiosi who secured votes for them. It marked the first time that Sicilian citizens had taken such a stand against the Mafia.
>
> (Baldassaro 2015: 103)

Among the names Dolci mentioned on that occasion there were also Calogero Volpe, Bernardo Mattarella and Girolamo Messeri, who at the time were respectively the Undersecretary of Health, the Minister of Foreign Trade, and a Senator of the Republic.

The complaint resulted in a trial against Dolci and Alasia, who were accused of defamation. Following the decision in both the first inquiry and the appeal to not hear all the defense witnesses, the defendants decided to revoke their lawyers' mandate and thereby give up their defense as a sign of protest against a trial they considered unfair. When the trial ended, Dolci and Alasia had each been sentenced to two years and nineteen months in jail, but it was suspended. Nevertheless, Mattarella lost his ministerial position with the formation of the new government headed by Aldo Moro in 1966.

Besides being a political activist, Dolci was an educator. In particular, starting in the 1970s, he began his educational work in Partinico by creating a Center for Alternative Education, with the aim of training future local community leaders. In fact, it was his firm belief that a town was poor and remained poor because its leaders were unable to understand how best to implement development initiatives.

He died on 30 December 1997 from a sudden phlebitis in his leg that provoked a stroke. As Galtung himself recalled in a 2001 speech in Palermo, reported by Bonora (2011: 272–78), Dolci's contributions to the sociology of peace and nonviolence were manifold:

*The scientific method*: All his nonviolent actions, social projects and reforms were preceded by a careful analysis of the data and by the use of the method of participant observation, by which sociologists immerse themselves for long periods in the environment and social group they intend to study, and describe the group members' actions to understand their motivations. The goal is to reconstruct the point of view of the group members and the rules (sometimes unexpressed) that underlie social inter-action within the community.

*Dialogue*: The need to ask questions is a very prominent aspect in Danilo's texts. It is a method by which it is possible to obtain an interlocutor's help to get an in-depth understanding of an empirical reality. It may also be a way to discover a potential, not-yet-achieved reality (Bonora 2011: 273–74).

*Maieutics*: Through dialogue, questions and popular self-analysis Danilo tried to bring out the hidden creativity that people did not know they had. It was a process of individual and community growth that did not employ pre-packaged solutions but found solutions within the social fabric.

*Essential needs*: Seen not only as economic needs, or needs related to consumption, but also and above all as the ability to gain the rights to free expression and participation in political and social life. Here it seems that Dolci anticipated in a certain sense the statements that Amartya Sen later made in *On Economic Inequality* (1973).

*The social network*: "For Danilo the main object of diagnostic analysis was the hierarchy and cronyism he had found in Italian (and not just Italian) pol-itics and in a very developed form in Sicily, in the gray area between official politics and the Mafia. Even the Mafiosi were *someone's* cronies" (Bonora 2011: 275). Dolci's purpose was to trace the path of cronyism, so as to understand how far it penetrated and where it began, studying the structural and cultural conditions that favored the spread of this social scourge.

*Nonviolent language*: As a poet and writer, he was able to use the Italian language to denounce in the most effective and at the same time elegant and intelligent manner the conditions of degradation he saw on a daily basis, without ever falling into verbal violence.

*Nonviolent action*: This is to be understood as a stage in reappropriation of people's personal dignity and future. The reverse strike was the highest expression of this legacy. It was undertaken to demand and build respect for Article 4 of the Italian Constitution.[4] This could only put into practice when basic needs had been understood through popular self-analysis and when the goals to be achieved were established.

Dolci's work as a sociologist, activist and reformer was an essential stage leading up to the contemporary study of techniques of nonviolence and theories of peace. Starting in the post-war period, a period dominated by the Cold War, ideologies and state bureaucratization, he succeeded in making known, through his denunciations, the poverty-stricken Sicily that had suffered through the two world wars – a Sicily abandoned to itself, suffocated by violence, patronage, the Mafia and ignorance. He had shown how a new, different way of conceiving society, politics and public institutions was possible and, through popular participation, programmed from the grass-roots level, a social and politico-institutional transformation of the reality in which he had chosen to live.

Dolci refounded the sociological, economic and political approaches for tackling the problems of underdevelopment, poverty and democratization, and worked to build a civil society capable of inventing innovative processes indispensable for effecting change.

## Notes

1  The concordat recognized the independence of the Holy See, which founded the Vatican State, a theocratic state with institutions independent of Italian ones. Italy also recognized huge reimbursements in favor of the Vatican State and its exemption from taxes and customs duties, recognized Catholicism as a state religion and established the teaching of the Catholic religion in schools.
2  The previous Italian currency.
3  The title refers to the first part of a popular Sicilian saying: "Cu ioca sulu a un' perdi mai" ("He who plays alone never loses"). But that player and game are not without rules: the player can win not because he plays alone but because he adjusts to the rules in order not to lose (Cambi and Staccioli 2007: 154).
4  The article reads: "The Republic recognizes that all citizens have the right to work and promotes the conditions that make this right effective. Every citizen has the duty to carry out, according to his/her possibilities and his/her own choice, any activity or function that contributes to the material or spiritual progress of society" (Bartolini 2006: 39).

## References

Angelico, B., and De Gennaro, R. (1991) Scusaci, maestro di pace. *La Repubblica – Torino*, 20 January, iii.

Baldassaro, L. (2015) Peace profile: Danilo Dolci. *Peace Review: A Journal of Social Justice* 27(1), 100–107.

Barone, G., and Mazzi, S., ed. (2008) *Aldo Capitini – Danilo Dolci: lettere 1952–1968*. Rome: Carocci Editore.

Bartolini, F. (2006) *Il Codice Civile e le leggi complementari*. Piacenza: Casa Editrice La Tribuna.

Bellamy, R., Ferrajoli, L., Negri, T., and Zolo, D. (2004) The legacy of Norberto Bobbio: assesments and recollections. *Critical Review of International Social and Political Philosophy* 7(3), 67–83.

Bentham, J. (1823) *A Fragment on Government; Or, a Comment on the Commentaries*. London: W. Pockering.

Bobbio, N. (1989) *Il terzo assente*. Torino: Sonda.

Bobbio, N. (1991a) Questa è legittima. *La Stampa*, 19 January, 7.

Bobbio, N. (1991b) Ci sono ancora guerre giuste? Me lo chiedo. *L'Unità*, 22 January, 1.

Bobbio, N. (1993) Questa volta dico no. *La Stampa*, 1 July, 1–2.

Bobbio, N. (1997) *Il problema della guerra e le vie della pace*. Bologna: Il Mulino.

Bobbio, N. (2004) *Autobiografia*. Bari: Editori Laterza.

Bobbio, N. (2011) *Il pensiero di Aldo Capitini: filosofia, religione, politica*. Rome: Edizioni dell'Asino.

Bonora, G. (2011) *Dolci richiami*. Ancona: Arduino Sacco Editore.

Cacciari, M. (1991) Quante sciocchezze a destra e a sinistra su questo conflitto. *L'Unità*, 18 January, 19.

Cambi, F., and Staccioli, G. (2007) *Il gioco in Occidente: storia, teorie, pratiche*. Rome: Armando Editore.

Capitini, A. (1942) *Vita Religiosa*. Bologna: Cappelli.

Capitini, A. (1947) *Saggio sul soggetto della storia*. Perugia: La Nuova Italia.

Capitini, A. (1950) *Nuova socialità e riforma religiosa*. Torino: Einaudi.

Capitini, A. (1955) *Religione aperta*. Parma: Guanda.

Capitini, A. (1960) La mia opposizione al fascismo. *Il Ponte* 16(1), 32–43.

Capini, A. (2009) *Le tecniche della nonviolenza*. Rome: Edizioni dell'Asino.

Carter, A. (1992) *Peace Movements: International Protest and World Politics since 1945*. New York: Routledge.

Deaglio, E. (1993) *Racconto rosso: la mafia, l'Italia e poi venne giù tutto*. Milano: Feltrinelli Editore.

Del Noce, A. (1968) Introduzione. In WeilS., *L'Amore di Dio*. Torino: Borla.

Dolci, D. (1954) *Fare presto (e bene) perché si muore*. Torino: De Silva.

Dolci, D. (1960) *Spreco: documenti e inchieste su alcuni aspetti dello spreco nella Sicilia occidentale*. Torino: Einaudi.

Dolci, D. (2009) *Banditi a Partinico*. Palermo: Sellerio.

Drago, A. (2007) The birth of nonviolence as a political theory. *Gandhi Marg* 29(3), 275–295.

Drago, A. (2014) Peace Profile: Aldo Capitini. *Peace Review* 26(3), 434–439.

Kramer, A. (2013) *Conscientious Objectors of the Second World War: Refusing to Fight*. Barnsley: Pen & Sword Social History.

Kelsen, H. (2007) *Peace through Law*. Clark: Lawbook Exchange.

Laurenti, M. C. (2007) *Simone Weil tra politica, filosofia e mistica*. Rome: Anicia.

Losurdo, D. (2010) *La non-violenza: una storia fuori dal mito*. Bari: Laterza.

Luporini, C. (1991) La guerra giusta? Un concetto inapplicabile: rischiamo la barbarie. *L'Unità*, 19 January, 14.

Mancini, M. (2009) *Stato di guerra e conflitto armato nel diritto internazionale*. Torino: G. Giappichelli Editore.

Mencaroni, L., ed. (1999) La vita di Aldo Capitini religioso, antifascista, vegetariano, nonviolento. *Azione Nonviolenta* 12, 2–5.

Parodi, G. (2012) Guido Calogero dal liberalsocialismo al riformismo. *Etica & Politica / Ethics & Politics*. 14(1), 344–464

Pierce, R. (1962) Sociology and utopia: the early writings of Simone Weil. *Political Science Quarterly* 77(4), 505–525.

Pétrement, S. (1994) *Vita di Simone Weil*. Milano: Adelphi.

Petricioli, M., and Cherubini, D., eds. (2007) *Pour la Paix en Europe: Institutions et société civile dans l'entre-deux-guerres/For Peace in Europe: Institutions and Civil Society between the World Wars*. Brussels: P.I.E. Peter Lang.

Ragone, M. (2011) *Le parole di Danilo Dolci: anatomia lessicale-concettuale*. Foggia: Edizioni del Rosone.

Schell, J. (1982) *The Fate of the Earth*. New York: Knopf.

Vigilante, A. (2012) *Ecologia del potere: studio su Danilo Dolci*. Foggia: Edizioni del Rosone, <http://educazioneaperta.it/wp-content/uploads/2017/04/Antonio_Vigilante_Ecologia_del_potere.pdf> (accessed 14 July 2017).

Weil, S. (1974) *La Grecia e le intuizioni precristiane*. Milano: Rusconi Editore.

Weil, S. (1999) Sulla Germania totalitaria. In Gaeta, G., ed., *Sulla Germania totalitaria*. Milano: Adelphi.

Weil, S. (2002) *Riflessioni sulla Guerra*. Milano: Adelphiana, <http://www.gianfrancobertagni.it/materiali/weil/riflessioniguerra.pdf> (accessed 14 July 2017).

Weil, S. (2004) *Oppression and Liberty*. London: Routledge.

Weil, S. (2005) *Sulla guerra: scritti 1933–1943*. Milano: Nuove Edizioni Tascabili.

Young, N. (1986) The peace movement: a comparative and analytical survey. *Alternatives: Global, Local, Political* 11(2), 185–217.

Zangrandi, R. (1964) *Il lungo viaggio attraverso il fascismo*. Milano: Feltrinelli.

Zolo, D. (1991) Che differenza c'è tra "guerra giusta" e "Allah Akbar." *L'Unità*, 22 January, 13.

Zolo, D. (2008) *L'Alito della libertà*. Milano: Feltrinelli.

# 3 The origins of academic peace research

## Peace research enters the academia

After a deep excursus on the philosophical and sociological roots of the first approaches to nonviolence and peace, it is now time to consider how – in a sociological perspective – the institutionalization of peace-and-nonviolence research started. We will then see how, starting from the late 1950s, the first research institutes, both university and not, were created for the study of conflicts, nonviolence and peace, and how the first avenues of research and degree programs spread. It is a deeply interdisciplinary field including dialogue on the most suitable methodologies to be used in this discipline.

Based on historical data on the creation of the first departments and the first scientific reviews, we can state that peace studies became an independent discipline only after the Second World War. Though between the First and Second World Wars authors such as Lewis Fry Richardson,[1] Quincy Wright,[2] David Mitrany[3] and Pitirim Sorokin[4] had laid the foundation for these developments through "studies on conflict management, war frequency and *peace making*" (Kriesberg 2010: 427), it was only in 1945 that the first French Institute of Polemology (Institut Français de Polémologie) was founded in France – more precisely in Paris – on the initiative of Gaston Bouthoul. The institute aimed at providing a very analytical and sociological study of the war. Therefore, the peculiar feature of the work by Bouthoul was a deep interdisciplinarity and it considered not only the technico-historical aspects of conflicts, but also the economical, psychological and social aspects of war as a collective phenomenon (Bouthoul 1963).

His approach, particularly Durkheimian, leads him to highlight the aspects of the "collective fervor" of conflicts, their irruption in real time by breaking its flow, increasing the intensity of social relationships and communication flows; this is where his certainty about the not totally rational and voluntary nature of war and the inability of legal measures (such as international rights) to control it come from. Nonetheless, and for this reason, he gives it the important task of getting this plague away from mankind; this is only possible by identifying equivalent functions to those of the phenomena of war, matching the study of the causes of war with a scientific analysis of its functions, according to the methodological track discovered by Durkheim for the study of social phenomena.

(Maniscalco 2010: 43)

Despite Bouthoul's and the French Institute of Polemology's main object of study being war rather than peace, in *Psicoanalisi della guerra* (Psychoanalysis of war) Franco Fornari (1966) highlights that Bouthoul's aim

is *peace research*, namely scientific research not disinterested in its purpose, but willing since its very beginning to investigate the conditions of survival in the historical moment when, due to the application of scientific research results, survival is impaired.

(Fornari 1969: 20)

Up to that moment, the main approach in studies of peace had been complementary to the methodological requirements of the "realist" school of international politics. Many scholars were therefore starting to understand the need to change their own points of view, with a focus on collective phenomena.

We shall now go back to consideration of the context of destruction left by the Second World War. The end of the two world wars had led to the counting of bodies and damages, to the prosecution of the guilty, to reconstruction and, in the scientific field, to the desire to avoid, no matter what, the outbreak of a new, more disastrous total conflict. The weak balance of Cold War powers shifted the attention of scientists and activists to the disarmament issue and the dangers of scientific research conducted for the sake of war. The *Russell–Einstein Manifesto* (1955) and the founding of the Pugwash Conferences on Science and World Affairs (1957) were a clear consequence of this desire.

The document by Russell and Einstein contains all the concerns raised by many scientists on the nuclear danger:

In the tragic situation which confronts humanity, we feel that scientists should assemble in conference to appraise the perils that have arisen as a result of the development of weapons of mass destruction, and to discuss a resolution in the spirit of the appended draft.

We are speaking on this occasion, not as members of this or that nation, continent, or creed, but as human beings, members of the species Man, whose continued existence is in doubt. The world is full of conflicts; and, overshadowing all minor conflicts, the titanic struggle between Communism and anti-Communism.

Almost everybody who is politically conscious has strong feelings about one or more of these issues; but we want you, if you can, to set aside such feelings and consider yourselves only as members of a biological species which has had a remarkable history, and whose disappearance none of us can desire.

We shall try to say no single word which should appeal to one group rather than to another. All, equally, are in peril, and, if the peril is understood, there is hope that they may collectively avert it.

We have to learn to think in a new way. We have to learn to ask ourselves, not what steps can be taken to give military victory to whatever group we prefer, for there no longer are such steps; the question we have to ask ourselves is: what steps can be taken to prevent a military contest of which the issue must be disastrous to all parties?

(Butcher 2005: 25)

The fundamental dilemma emphasized by the *Manifesto* was contained in a question: "Shall we put an end to the human race; or shall mankind renounce war?" (Bucher 2005: 26). These declarations and the fact that they highlighted the ill effects that the use of nuclear weapons could have on humankind's survival pushed scientists worldwide to take action against war. Such action would come two years later through the Pugwash Conferences. It was a meeting strongly wished for, not only by Einstein and Russell, but also by Jawaharlal Nehru, Eugene Rabinowitch (from the Federation of American Scientists), and Joseph Rotblat (from the British Atomic Scientists' Association) and aimed at the "institution of a committee of scientists to explain to the world the effect a nuclear war would have on humanity as a whole" (Rotblat 1967: 11).

For this reason, the British Atomic Scientists' Association founded a study team to establish the International Conference on Science and Society. This led Rabinowitch and Rotblat to meet several times in London between 1954 and 1955 to discuss the idea of including even Russians in this plan (Rotblat 1972: 1). The participation of Rabinowitch and Alexander Topchiev in the conference organized by the World Association of Parliamentarians for World Government in 1955 represented a crucial moment for dialogue between scholars coming from two opposite contexts. Indeed, Topchiev was a high official from the Soviet Academy of Science and would later become the leader of the Soviet Pugwash group (Rotblat 1962: 5).

The investigative fields on which the Pugwash Conference focused where mainly three: the evaluation of the consequences of the development of nuclear energy and weapons, the disarmament issues, and the social responsibilities of scientists.

Even in Japan, the nation that had already experienced more than any other country the dangers of nuclear arms, anti-nuclear feelings began to swell. During the 1950s even the decision makers were influenced by such feelings.

Japanese anti-nuclear feelings started crystallizing in 1954, when some Japanese fishermen on board the *Lucky Dragon* were highly contaminated (one was even killed) by the radioactive rain released by an American nuclear test made on Bikini Atoll. The episode galvanized public opinion and caused a storm of anti-nuclear protest. Almost 20 million people signed petitions asking for disarmament and for the end of nuclear tests.

> Both the upper and lower chambers of Parliament adopted unanimous resolutions calling for a ban on nuclear weapons. Most prefectural governments and some 250 municipalities passed similar resolutions. For the first time in Japanese history the peace movement gained widespread support and respectability within society and was able to influence government decision makers.
>
> (Cortright 2008: 138)

As we saw in the previous chapter, the original contributions of Norberto Bobbio to debates on the dangers of war and the desire for peace were born in this delicate historico-political and cultural world phase. Bobbio rediscovered and emphasized, more than anybody else, the importance of the integration of states, starting what he himself used to call *institutional* (or *juridical*) pacifism foreseeing, among other things, the creation of an international organization capable of holding a legitimate monopoly on violence.

For those, like Bobbio, who considered it realistic to be a "pessimist"[5] there could be no other remedy for war than an "intelligent despair" leading us to meditate on how to save ourselves. And safety, for Bobbio, should be obtained by the reform of international institutions able to exercise, even as far as relations between states were concerned, the Hobbesean principle of the "monopoly of force."

As highlighted in the issues treated by the scholars of that time, the impetus to research on peace was rooted in the fear of a new nuclear war and in the need to prevent further conflicts capable of devastating the human species. The Cold War and the equilibrium of terror then constituted the main rationale for peace research at a time when research mainly focused on the issues of disarmament, conflict theory and conflict analysis.

Though, as we saw, many conferences were organized by researchers of many scientific fields, there is no doubt that from the very beginning peace studies anchored themselves in the sphere of the social sciences. Interest in peace issues in the European social sciences was even more evident when, in 1952, the Oslo Institute for Social Research held a competition for essays on the "importance of scientific research for the peaceful resolution of international conflicts," to be included in a volume edited by Quincy Wright, Fred W. Cottrell and Charles Boasson.[6] The proposals for further research contained in the winning essays contributed to the creation, in 1959, of a section of the Oslo Institute for Social Research for research on conflicts and peace under the direction of Johan Galtung (Bobbio *et al.* 2004: 661).

In the same year, the Lancaster Peace Research Centre (now the Richardson Institute) was founded in Britain and starting from 1964, in Oslo, at the department for research on peace of the Oslo Institute for Social Research, the *Journal of Peace Research* started being published. In 1966 the Oslo department was turned into a research institute and called the Peace Research Institute of Oslo. "Starting from this moment, PRIO [the Peace Research Institute of Oslo] was a sort of launch platform for the first generation of peace researchers in Northern countries, and for young researchers in other countries" (Venturi 2013: 42), furthermore, it was one of the first centers aimed at studying "positive peace" as theorized by Galtung himself.[7]

In the same year, the Stockholm International Peace Research Institute, focusing on more traditional research on arming, disarming and international security, was founded in Stockholm. Starting from 1969, the Institute published an important yearly report, the *SIPRI Yearbook: Armaments, Disarmament and International Security*, aimed at spreading data, surveys and impartial research on the impacts of military expenditures on the international community, on arms control and on regional and international security.

Even in the American context there were interesting developments in peace research through the creation of the Center for Research on Conflict Resolution at Michigan University in 1959.[8]

> In 1957 the *Journal of Conflict Resolution*, the first review for research on conflicts and peace, which, as time went by more and more dealt with the application of game theory to conflict studies, had already been founded at the same university. Among the most active collaborators in such initiatives, there were the economist K. Boulding, the sociologist R. Angell, the psychologist D. Katz and the mathematician and biologist A. Rapoport.
>
> (Bobbio 2004: 661)

The 1960s were also the period when the first associations of peace researchers were born. In 1963, on the initiative of Walter Isard, the Peace Research Society (International), afterwards renamed the Peace Science Society (International), was created and in 1964 the International Peace Research Association was founded. In 1966 it started publishing the bulletin the *International Peace Research Newsletter*, where info about peace research on a global level was issued.

The institutionalization of peace research, and the spreading of yearly reports, reports, journals, reviews and newsletters, was also a sign of the growing respectability of peace research. This was the passage from "movement" to "science." As "science," peace research supported the instruments of applied research, which was different from activism; such research strictly applied analytical methods and theoretical models to political issues and tried to check the results in the widest way possible to create a dynamic social science (Chatfield 1979: 170).

## Research paradigms and methodologies between the 1950s and early 1960s

As previously highlighted, the rise of research institutes both in Europe and the United States during 1950s and 1960s went hand in hand with the development of debates on research methods in peace research as a social science and of the principles at the basis of the social sciences themselves. This led to the rise of two currents of research in the study of these phenomena within the behavioral approach: one of these built up conflict issues and the other peace issues as a foundation.

Examples of the first research current were the Center for Advanced Studies on the Behavioral Sciences, started in 1954 in Palo Alto, California, and the *Journal of Conflict Resolution* (1957) at the University of Michigan. Both of these initiatives were supported by the group of Kelman, Rapoport, Boulding and Richardson involving specialists, particularly in international relations (Venturi 2013: 40), and staying anchored in the realism typical of traditional methodology.

The behavioral approach began to be so much followed as to start a strong debate among international scholars between "traditionalism" and "behaviorism" (Kaplan 1966).

While most traditionalists based their study-and-research methodology on interpretations of history and philosophy of law in ways that recalled the concepts of classical political philosophy, the behaviorists based theirs on a conception of research more empirical and more based on the political and social reality. And while the former referred to the paradigms of qualitative research, the latter worked using the instruments of quantitative research and interpretations of the causality of human action.

The debate stimulated by behaviorist theories of conflict had an important role in the rise of a specific strand of research: the behaviorist study of peace, which found its expression in Europe, namely in Oslo, with the formation, on the initiative of Johan Galtung, of the Peace Research Institute of Oslo (1959) and afterwards the *Journal of Peace Research* (1964):

> The choice of "conflict" in Michigan and "peace" in Oslo reflects the controversy surrounding the word "peace." Not only were "Peace" movements seen, at the time, as upholding Soviet interests, but "peace" also was perceived as detached from the "hard politics" of conflicts. Institutes ever since would opt for a focus on peace and/or conflict, often reflected in their designation.
>
> (Sousa 2017: 9–10)

It is also interesting to remember that the choice, by research centers and reviews, to use the word "conflict" instead of "peace" in their names was often due to the fact that "'conflict' was more established as an academic term" (Gledisch *et al.* 2014: 147), and to the fact that many people thought that "peace" reminded them of socialist pacifism fighting for liberty, equality and justice in international relations while maintaining limited rights of liberty within socialist states, or that the word "'peace' seemed to be a word too much abused these days» (Anon. 1957: 2). For these reasons, many research institutes decided to talk of "peace and conflict" or "peace and development" looking for a compromise.

## The development of research methods between late 1960s and 1980s

Although activists and peace researchers were allies in the struggle for the term "peace research," relations between them eventually soured. Just as the behavioral revolution was taking hold in sociology and political science, the student revolt occurred, first in Berkley in 1964 and then in Europe from 1968 on. The liberationist, even anarchist, tone of the first insurgencies at the universities sounded a note that was superficially favorable to peace, epitomized in the slogan "Make Love Not War." But the student revolutionaries were not enamored by things American, including "American social science." The behaviorist tone of much of peace research became a source of suspicion, and so did its "neutral" stand on the East–West conflict. Many, including some young peace researchers, turned to Marxism (mostly the Maoist rather than the Soviet variety) and the liberation eventually turned into dogma and strong support for violence.

(Gleditsch *et al.* 2014: 147–48)

This was the period in which Johan Galtung included the concept of "structural violence" in his distinction between "negative" and "positive" peace" first issued in 1964 (Galtung 1964). In his article "Violence, Peace and Peace Research" (1969) he muddied the waters drawing attention from the political contraposition of East and West to violence as a social problem resulting from the organization of society itself. Though the original intention of this new concept was to make people think of economic disparities, it was afterwards linked to another kind of violence, namely "cultural violence," able to justify some dysfunctions among the political and social institutions and strengthen some conditions of "structural violence."

The introduction of the concept of structural violence brought about a radical change in the way conflicts were studied and researched. Attention was for the first time drawn from the state to the individual (Sousa 2017: 10), restoring the latter's place at the center of the systems.

Two further currents then arose within European peace research: one was guided by Norwegian sociologist Galtung, who pushed peace research towards the elimination of violence in all its forms; and the other, guided by Schmidt who, just like Marx, thought that in certain situations – namely where justice was totally on one side and injustice on the other, such as in the relationship of slaves and slavers – reconciliation and mediation could be useless and there was a clear need to use violence to win the conflict and make social justice a reality (Schmidt 1968; Fossati 1986).

While the 1970s were a period of stasis, starting from the 1980s, when the danger of nuclear war, the contraposition of blocks, and the risks of a power imbalance in favor of either the United States or of the USSR were felt again, peace research was again discussed. Though the contraposition of currents persisted, there is no doubt that the study of negative peace overwhelmed that of the positive, and of structural violence. Furthermore, due to the air of emergency that featured in these studies, less attention and less concern attached to both the methodological aspects and the justification of methodology itself (Gleditsch 2014: 150).

Nonetheless, as Fossati highlights, the peace researchers closest to the positive-peace orientation started to think once more about security and disarmament problems and theorized for the first time the concept of "trans-armament," that is to say the transformation of the opposition between armed and non-armed intervention from an *aut–aut* (either–or) into a functional distinction that can be summarized in *et–et* (and–and) (Maniscalco 2010: 151):

> Peace researchers [...] (with Galtung 1984) created the concept of "trans-armament," which referred to European defensive models based on making weapons and defense strategies "defensive" rather than offensive. Some researchers hoped for an evolution towards non-violent popular defense models. Peace research scholars ended up dialoguing with the remaining European (mostly English and German) social democratic parties. The Italian political context was far removed from such debate: both on the demand – the "communist" side was indeed oriented towards the values of movementist manicheism – and on the offer front – the only exception was that of research promoted by the Florence forum on peace and war issues.
>
> (Fossati 2001: 16)

With the fall of Berlin Wall, 1989 represented a crucial year for the new weakening of peace research, since if, on one hand, it abolished remaining international conflicts thanks to the progressive weakening and subsequent collapse of the USSR and its ideological dogmas, on the other the scenario laying ahead let Western governments think that in future there would be fewer conflict threats.

Although it may be said that the number of conflicts has increased since then, it is equally possible to confirm that the threats perceived in the West in relation to these conflicts have been very limited. Here then is the reason why, starting from 1989, the problems of peace, war and nonviolent methods of conflict management have become secondary subjects compared with those of economic development, globalization and democratization processes.

Since 1989 peace finally ceased being an absolute value because the nuclear danger ceased and with it the risk of the extinction of humanity. The debates focus again on three important values to be defended and which can certainly be traced back to the concept of positive peace Galtung spoke of in 1969: democracy, the market and the right of self-determination of peoples. This shift towards the problems of democracy, the market and self-determination could in a sense be considered a confirmation of Galtung's intuition: "the value of peace (absence of war) is insufficient to motivate the efforts of a generation of scholars to help change politics" (Fossati 2001: 17).

## Notes

1 Lewis Fry Richardson was among the pioneers of peace studies. During his life he wrote many articles for academic reviews on war-and-peace issues, but it was

only with his two posthumously published books – *Arms and Insecurity: A Mathematical Study of the Causes and Origins of War* and *Statistics of Deadly Quarrels* – published in 1960 that many of his ideas on such themes became accessible and he was fully recognized as a precursor of this subject.

2 At the end of the Second World War, the attention of sociologists and political scientists focused on new methods to prevent further world conflicts. Quincy Wright's academic activity is fully part of this line of research and makes extraordinary contributions to the understanding of conflicts. Starting from 1920, in fact, Wright began a study of the wars that led him to publish more than forty scientific articles and ten books. The results of this immense work were synthesized and systematized in *A Study of War* (1942), one of the most complete examples of quantitative research ever conducted on the topic of war. In it the author examined the institution of war in historical, cultural and legal perspectives and concluded that war could be prevented through the creation of a world institution that had adequate power over nation states.

3 Mitrany's contribution to the debate on conflict prevention concerns what he himself calls "institutional functionalism." Aware of the criticisms by federal systems, he called for the creation of international organizations specific to specific functions. These are institutions subject to particular conditions and limits established by their statutes.

4 Sorokin believed that sociologists spend too much time studying the destructive aspects of human behavior instead of focusing their attention on the productive ones. For this reason, he began his studies on altruism. The third of the four volumes of *Social and Cultural Dynamics* (as amended in 1956) offers interesting perspectives on the quantitative study of conflicts. "This significant part of the work contains statistics on wars and battles from the sixth century BC until the 1920s. Sorokin's attention is focused on researching how history creates multiple empirical indicators. Among these, one of the most important results of the research is to verify that no type of culture is, internally or externally, more belligerent than another. Almost a thousand wars are analyzed in the text, comparing data and quantitative aspects: the strength of the armies, the number of losses and the duration of each war are studied in their complexity. The different historical eras are compared, and wars are pondered in their effects in comparison with the number of inhabitants in the involved populations. In this way, Sorokin finds that periods of the most intense war have been those of transition from one cultural domain to another, while there is no consistent tendency towards the disappearance or decrease of war" (Venturi 2013: 30).

5 "We cannot, we must not be optimistic. Today, the optimist is the one who, with sincerity, without false idols, has renounced the reality of the world in which he lives. I am not saying that we should bow to the pessimists. But at least the pessimists have the advantage of hard-and-fast proof drawn from life and history, and because it is difficult to accept, they urge us to think, to save ourselves, to work for salvation without illusions. An attitude of intelligent despair is better than the opposite attitude of obtuse hope" (Bobbio 1997: 24).

6 Award-winning texts were published in Wright *et al.* 1954.

7 For the distinction between positive and negative peace, see "Conflict Theory and the Method of Transcendence," in Chapter 4.

8 As Kenneth Boulding reports, the Center had to be named after the research on peace, but to avoid misunderstandings and to stay more in keeping with the political line of the decision makers of that period, which was entirely devoted to the

implementation of research on conflicts, security and disarmament. "Peace is a word of so many meanings that one hesitates to use it for fear of being misunderstood. When, for instance, a group of us set up the Center for Conflict Resolution at the University of Michigan in 1956, we conceived it as a center for peace research, but we deliberately avoided the use of the word 'peace' in the title because of the misunderstandings that might arise" (Boulding 1978: 3).

# References

Anon. (1957) An editorial. *Conflict Resolution* 1(1), 1–3.
Bobbio, N. (1997) *Il problema della guerra e le vie della pace*. Bologna: Il Mulino.
Bobbio, N., MatteucciN., and PasquinoG. (2004) *Il Dizionario di Politica*. Torino: Utet.
Boulding, K. E. (1978) *Stable Peace*. Austin and London: University of Texas Press.
Bouthoul, G. (1963) *War*. New York: Walker.
Butcher, S. I. (2005) The origins of the *Russell–Einstein Manifesto*. Pugwash History Series 1. Pugwash Conferences on Science and World Affairs, <https://pugwashconferences.files.wordpress.com/2014/02/2005_history_origins_of_manifesto3.pdf> (accessed 27 July 2017).
Chatfield, C. (1979) International peace research: the field defined by dissemination. *Journal of Peace Research* 16(2), 163–179.
Cortright, D. (2008) *Peace: A history of Movements and Ideas*. Cambridge: Cambridge University Press.
Fornari, F. (1966) *Psicoanalisi della guerra*. Milano: Feltrinelli.
Fornari, F. (1969) *Dissacrazione della guerra – dal pacifismo alla scienza dei conflitti*. Milano: Feltrinelli.
Fossati, F. (1986) Sviluppo e dibattiti nella peace research attraverso le conferenze dell'Ipra. *Progetto Pace* 1(1), 95–106
Fossati, F. (2001) Introduzione alla peace research. In Licata, A., ed., *Università per la pace*. Gorizia: Istituto di Sociologia Internazionale, 15–22.
[Galtung, J.] (1964) An editorial: what is peace research? *Journal of Peace Research* 1(1), 1–4.
Galtung, J. (1969). Violence, peace and peace research. *Journal of Peace Research* 6(3), 167–191.
Gleditsch, N. P., Nordkwelle, J., and Strand, H. (2014) Peace research – just the study of war? *Journal of Peace Research* 51(2), 145–158.
Kaplan, M. (1966) The new great debate: traditionalism vs science in international relations. *World Politics* 19(1), 1–20.
Kriesberg, L. (2010) Conflict resolution: an overview. In Young, N., ed., *The Oxford International Encyclopedia of Peace*. Oxford: Oxford University Press, 427–431.
Maniscalco, M. L. (2010) *Sociologia dei conflitti: dai classici alla peace research*. Matera: Diòtima.
Rotblat, J. (1962) *Science and World Affairs: History of the Pugwash Conferences*. London: Dawsons of Pall Mall.

Rotblat, J. (1967) *Pugwash: A History of the Pugwash Conferences on Science and World Affairs*. Prague: Czechoslovak Academy of Sciences.

Rotblat, J. (1972) *Scientists in the Quest for Peace*. Cambridge, MA: MIT Press.

Schmidt, H. (1968) Politics and peace research. *Journal of Peace Research* 3(5), 217–232.

Sousa, R. R. P. (2017) Genealogy of behaviourist peace research. *JANUS.NET e-journal of International Relations* 8(1), <http://hdl.handle.net/11144/3030> (accessed 27 July 2017).

Venturi, B. (2013) *Il demone della pace: storia, metodologie e prospettive istitu-zionali della peace research e del pensiero di Johan Galtung*. Bologna: I Libri di Emil.

Wright, Q., Cottrell, F. W., and Boasson, C. (1954) *Research for Peace*. Amsterdam: North-Holland Publishing Co.

# 4　The sociological peace research of Johan Galtung

## Life and theoretical influences

"There are some people like Picasso whose output is so large and so varied that it is hard to believe that it comes from only one person. Johan Galtung falls into this category" (Boulding 1977: 75). As the experts from this sector know, contributions to peace research by Johan Galtung from the sociological perspective were huge, holistic and connected to more than twenty further disciplines dealing with the social sciences. Among the most important contributions, we must remember: the concepts of positive peace and negative peace; the concepts of direct, structural and cultural violence; theories of peace, conflict, development and civilization; negotiation, mediation, the "transcend" method; peace economics; peace education; and the methodologies of social research.

Born in Oslo in 1930, as years went by Johan Galtung became the founder of peace research as a discipline at an academic level. He was a negotiator on behalf of the United Nations, a professor and deeply knowledgeable of conflict dynamics. In 1959, he founded the Peace Research Institute of Oslo, in 1964 the *Journal of Peace Research*, in 1993 the Transcend Peace University, in 2011 the Galtung Institute for Peace Theory and Peace Practice in Germany, and in 2012 the Hardanger Academy for Peace, Development and Environment in Norway. It is therefore clear that education and the dissemination of knowledge has had weight in his thinking and his life and career.

Born to an aristocratic Norwegian family, Galtung was the son of a doctor and lived under the Nazi invasion from 9 April to 10 June 1940. As he himself stated in an autobiography (Galtung 2000), despite helping some German soldiers wounded during an accident (he did not care about the fact that they were his enemies), his father was deported to a death camp. He was so lucky as to go back home one month before the war ended and manage to survive the experience of the camp. The impact these events had on young Galtung was so strong he afterwards decided to commit his life to the prevention of war and to nonviolence. Such interests had already arisen during his time at university, when he was simultaneously studying for a degree in mathematics and for another one in sociology.

After completing university studies, Galtung was called to military service but declared himself a conscientious objector. He was arrested and held in a jail for six months:

> Those months were, as well as for Gramsci and Gandhi, an occasion to study and write. Guided by Arne Næss, he got interested in the study of *satyagraha*, the Gandhian fighting method that set an inseparable link between the means and ends of political action.
>
> (Altieri 2008: 8)

Arne Næss was his first master and the one who introduced him to the study of Gandhian ethics. The results of such a community of views and interests are contained in a Norwegian publication (never translated into other languages) dating back to 1955,[1] whose title could be translated into English as *Political Ethics of Gandhi*. It becomes hence clear that, since the very beginning, his thought was deeply rooted in Gandhian ethics and nonviolence. The latter will be the characteristic *fil rouge* resurfacing in all further publications by Galtung.

The contact he had with Danilo Dolci in Sicily is interesting as well. Altieri explains it as follows:

> Between 1956 and 1957 he went to Sicily to study the situation of that land and support the nonviolent work of Danilo Dolci, the Sicilian Gandhi, who had started a huge program of denouncments and positive actions (the "reversed strike" was an example) to fight the Mafiosi, the institutional as well as the direct violence leading adults to forced unemployment and children to death by starvation. [...] The Sicilian experience was ignored by his biographers.
>
> (Altieri 2008: 8–9)

The importance of Sicily for Galtung can also be seen in "Dolci Richiami: testimonianze di familiari, amici e collaboratori su Danilo Dolci" (Sweet reminiscence: testimonies of family, friends and colleagues on Danilo Dolci) by Giovanni Bonora (2011), where Galtung explains: "I think Danilo was one of the most important Italians who lived in the last century. The other one is Gramsci. They were both writers. They were both in prison. The third one is Norberto Bobbio" (Bonora 2011: 270).

Dolci influenced the thought of the young Galtung to such an extent that many of the studies by the latter reflected his teachings. Consider for example the holistic approach and the interdisciplinary thinking of both, the scientific method, the study of social phenomena, the attention to *basic needs*, the tendency towards eco-politics and eco-development, the attempt to transform and transcend conflicts, the classification of types of violence, the importance of education and so on. The Partinico of the 1950s and 1960s and the methods that Dolci applied in that disadvantaged context would form the basis of the theoretical system that his colleague and friend Galtung would develop in the 1970s.

After Sicily, another journey is crucial to the genesis of Galtung's thought: the period he spent at Columbia University in 1958. Here, besides getting interested in racial conflicts and how to transform them, he met Robert K. Merton and Pitrim A. Sorokin. Reviving Mertonian structural functionalism, Galtung came to elaborate a structural theory of imperialism that considered two-way relations between social systems and between states. Galtung's notion of imperialism defined itself as a special type of domination of a collectivity (usually a nation) over another. At the base there was the mechanism through which the center of the imperialist nation established a bridgehead with the center of the domi-nated/peripheral nation through a harmony of interests. In its strongest form, the imperialist system was governed not by interests of moot benefit but by relations of power (occupation, invasion, etc.) with one or more peripheries.

The two main mechanisms of action in the imperialistic system were thus identified. One is the vertical interaction model, based on which the dominating nation gets richer more quickly through a downwardly orien-ted process of interaction with the dominated nation. The second is the feudal interaction model, in which peripheral nations that are subject to imperialistic dominion are separated and kept in a condition of poor com-munication and poor mutual exchange (Galtung 1971).

After going back to Norway – as already mentioned – in 1959, Galtung founded the Peace Research Institute of Oslo and the *Journal of Peace Research* in 1964.

Among the various trips that he afterwards made around the world, we should recall the one to Africa in 1965, where he went to collect information on apartheid in Rhodesia that was fundamental for the devel-opment of the theory of structural violence. And the one to India in 1969. Here, Galtung for the first time distinguished the three types of violence: "direct," "structural" and "cultural" (Galtung 1969).

As acknowledged by Boulding himself in "Twelve Friendly Quarrels with Johan Galtung" (1977) the work done by our author is so wide and varied we hardly believe it issued from just one person. Let's consider his main contributions in the following paragraphs.

## Diagnosis, prognosis and therapy: medical science as a model for social research

In *Peace by Peaceful Means: Peace and Conflict, Development and Civilization* (1996), one of his most important studies, Galtung explains that

> peace studies are so similar to health studies that the triangle diagnosis–prognosis–therapy can be applied. There is the common idea of a system (of actors, of cells), of well-states and ill-states. The word-pairs "health/disease" from health studies and "peace/violence" from peace studies can be seen as specifications of these more general labels.
>
> (Galtung 1996: 1)

In this sense, Galtung notes that there are parallels between medical and social science because both have to deal with states of well-being, defined health conditions, and states of discomfort, defined states of disease. If in medicine the state of well-being corresponds to a stable balance of the key parameters of the human body, in the same way a condition of peace is probably likewise a condition of relational balance. Given these similarities, the moments of diagnosis, prognosis and therapy are necessary in both medical and social science.

Diagnosis is the moment when the researcher assesses the causes, conditions and contexts (symptoms) that the system presents. This is an action that the researcher can carry out both when the system is healthy and when it shows signs of illness. If during their study the researcher realized that the system showed signs of disease, then a prognosis saying whether the system was able to self-restore or an external intervention was needed to save the situation would be required. Finally, therapy was the moment when "deliberate efforts by Self or Other [are made] to move the system back again toward some well-state" (Galtung 1996: 1).

## Violence and peace theories

In one of his most important articles, "Violence, Peace and Peace Research" (1969), Galtung explains that peace is the absence of violence. Here are the reasons for this: (a) because it accords with how we commonly use the word peace, and (b) because it sets the parameters of a social order so widely that we can see many variations in it. This implies that to create "peace," violence must be reduced and/or avoided. So, if peace is the absence of violence, then what is violence? Seen from the point of view of those who suffer from it, "violence is present when human beings are so influenced that their actual somatic and mental achievements are below their potential" (Galtung 1969: 168). That is to say, violence is what favors the difference between the possible and the actual. It is what increases the "gap" or prevents it from being reduced or filled. On the other hand, if we consider violence on the side of those who practice it, on the active side, then it is here that we can distinguish three types of violence: direct violence, indirect or structural violence, and cultural violence.

Direct violence consists in killing or wounding another person.

Indirect or structural violence derives from the social structure itself. It is the result of a certain type of social organization and the profound inequalities within it. The two best-known forms of structural violence that our author identifies belong to both the political and the economic sphere and are repression and exploitation. Both in fact have an impact on body and mind and even if not intentionally, they produce negative effects on those who suffer them (Galtung 1996: 2).

In support of both direct and structural violence there is cultural violence that exploits symbolism, religions, ideologies, languages, arts, communication, science and education to legitimize direct and structural violence. Expressions of this type of violence are racism, sexism and the devaluation and persecution of "minority" cultures (Figure 1).

As we have seen, the discourses on violence are inextricably linked to those on peace. In particular, in relation to this last question, we note that

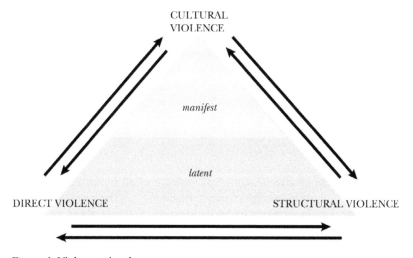

*Figure 1* Violence triangle.

the fundamental problem for theories of peace is defining and characterizing the concept of peace. In "Social Cosmology and the Concept of Peace" (Galtung 1981), after an historico-religious discourse investigating the concept of peace in different historical periods, and in heterogeneous geographical contexts (from the Roman to the Jewish, from the Indian to the Japanese) Galtung sets out what he thinks are the main historico-political and religious traditions:

a    In most cases the concept of peace was conceived – in a very limiting and partial way – as *pactum* and *absentia belli*, whose fundamental function remained that of consolidating the status quo. A peace that certainly guaranteed more control of a state of war and that rewarded both from an economic point of view and from the point of view of political control.

b    The knowledge of the different theories of peace, from the Oriental to the Western, from the ancient, to the modern, to the contemporary, allows the widening of the fields and the domain of the term. Once the latter are expanded, and once we have identified a maximum concept of peace containing all possible positive and imaginable aspects, it is necessary to start to deconstruct it to arrive at a minimally necessary but general notion of peace.

c    To achieve these results, it is crucial to enrich the knowledge derived from studies of violence. For example, "if 'peace of mind' is included in the concept of peace, and if peace is interpreted as identity, as closeness to oneself and to others, to society and nature, to something above oneself [...], then all that can reduce or prevent identity becomes violence" (Galtung 1981: 199).

We need to complete the framework by recalling "Violence, Peace and Peace Research." Here Galtung distinguishes two kinds of peace: negative and positive. They are considered two sides of the same coin (Galtung 1969) since negative peace is described as the "absence of personal violence," while positive peace is described as "absence of structural violence" (Galtung 1969: 183).

Later on, in 1996, Galtung will come back to this distinction to specify two suitable definitions of peace:

Peace is the absence/reduction of violence of all kinds. Peace is non-violent and creative conflict transformation. [...] The first definition is violence-oriented; peace being its negation. To know about peace, we have to know about violence.

The second definition is conflict-oriented; peace is the context for conflicts to unfold non-violently and creatively. To know about peace, we have to know about conflict and how conflicts can be transformed, both non-violently and creatively. Obviously, this latter definition is more dynamic than the former.

Both definitions focus on human beings in a social setting. This makes peace studies a social science, and more particularly an applied social science.

(Galtung 1996: 9)

## Conflict theory and the transcend method

In addition to a theory of peace, the scholar also needed a theory of conflict in order to arrive at the cognitive tools necessary to understand the phenomenon and to control it. A theory of conflict is indispensable not only for development studies but also for peace studies. In particular, we must recognize that "deep inside every conflict lies a contradiction, something standing in the way of something else. A problem in other words" (Galtung 1996: 70).

In Galtung's understanding, conflict could be seen as a triangle (Figure 2) whose vertices are made up of *Behavior*, B, namely conduct, manner of acting; *Attitude* and *Assumption*, A, namely mental outlook and suppositions; and *Contradiction*, C, namely the opposition that was conflict's reason for being. Here contradiction is an incompatibility of the objectives of the parties involved, which could cause a mismatch between social values and social structure (e.g. an individual's goals are unmet by the structure of society). Note that in Galtung's thought conflict is essential to life, and life is essential to conflict. Furthermore, conflict shows an evident side corresponding to behavior and a hidden one made up of attitudes and contradictions.

In a symmetrical conflict (in terms of power), contradiction (C) is defined by the actors, by their interests and by the clash of the latter. In an asymmetric conflict, however, contradiction is outlined by the parties, their interrelation and the conflicts of interests inherent in their relationships. For what concerns attitude (A), this concept includes all perceptions on the part of both the other and oneself. These perceptions, right or wrong, could be either positive or negative, but in violent conflict the parties tend to develop humiliating stereotypes of the other that necessarily influence their attitudes through emotions such as fear, anger, bitterness and hate. The concept of attitude therefore includes emotional (feelings), cognitive (opinions) and conative (will) elements. And finally, for what concerns behavior (B), this includes cooperation or coercion, gestures indicating conciliation or animosity. All practices implemented in the event of violent conflict are characterized by threats, coercion and destructive attacks.

We could therefore say that contradiction represents the condition of incompatibility within the system and that the conflict is the result of the sum of attitude, behavior and contradiction. In other words: Conflict = A + B + C.

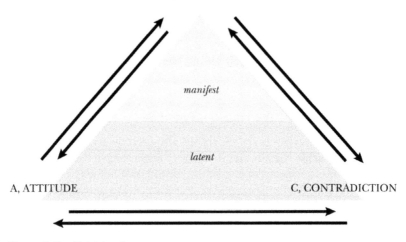

*Figure 2* Conflict triangle.

Conflict is therefore a dynamic process in which the three elements of the triangle are constantly engaged in influencing each other; the more dynamic the conflict, the more the contradictions and oppressions of parties become unsustainable. A spiral is developed in which parties adapt and organize to be able to pursue their interests, but in doing so assumed increasingly hostile attitudes and increasingly conflicting behavior. This is the way in which conflicts widen and intensy, often causing not only the entry into play of new parties but also the emergence of secondary conflicts linked to the main one.

As in the case of conflicts, Galtung also studied the dynamics of nonviolence and theorized a triangle of nonviolence superimposable on that of conflicts. As in the conflict triangle, that of nonviolence also consists of flows that go in six directions and represent relations between the vertices of a triangle (Figure 3).

Vertex A, which in the conflict triangle corresponds to *attitude*, in the triangle of nonviolence corresponds to the *empathy*:

> the ability to put yourself in the shoes of the other, to feel and perceive their emotions, to "see inside," to help; during the mediation process, the ability of the parties in conflict to free themselves from psychic ghosts that often prevent understanding what is really happening.
>
> (Salio 2016: 21)

The B vertex, which corresponds to *behavior* in the triangle of conflicts, in the triangle of nonviolence corresponds to the *nonviolence of action and dialogue.* These are in fact indispensable elements for preventing the degeneration of a conflict into violence:

> Dialogue is the tool that serves as a bridge between subjective aspects, attitudes, which characterize personal experience, and the emotional perceptions of conflicting objectives, and the more objective component constituted by real contradictions between the objectives that the parties intend to achieve.
>
> (Salio 2016: 21–22)

And finally, the C vertex, which in the triangle of conflicts corresponds to *contradiction*, in the triangle of nonviolence corresponds to *creativity.* Creativity is an indispensable requirement for the emergence of superior interests that unite parties rather than dividing them.

Taking advantage of knowledge gained about violence, peace, conflict and non-violence, Galtung recognizes that in traditional methods of managing and resolving conflicts there are problems or at least reasons for uncertainty. First, if the solution to a conflict consists in creating a new situation that is acceptable and sustainable for all the actors involved, then one can commonly assume that a conflict ends when the agreement is signed by the governors. However, this solution presents uncertainties related to the fact that signatories can choose to behave differently from what was agreed; or the fact that the signatories can choose to comply

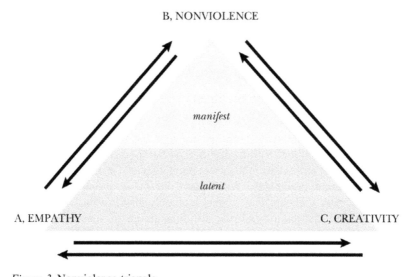

*Figure 3* Nonviolence triangle.

with the agreements made, but neglect the expressions of the base, of the people who can choose not to comply; or the fact that everyone can choose to respect the agreements, producing a new situation that is less conflictual, but there remains a risk of a new conflict breaking out as soon as any incorrect behavior ignites a residual grievance.

According to Galtung, these risks can only be overcome when the sustainability of the agreement is supported by endogenous approval, namely when it is supported and sedimented within society. In this perspective, the transformation of conflict is an endless process, and the objective is no longer a precise moment in history at which the conflict is considered resolved, but the process of transformation itself (Galtung 1996: 89–90). "The nonviolent transformation of the conflict is a constructive modality as it helps to find solutions that allow all the parties to obtain benefits and, consequently, the conflict becomes an opportunity for growth for everyone" (Salio 2016: 20). To achieve this, a creative approach to conflict is needed that can produce a new solution never before considered. By exploiting the positive aspects of conflict, dialogue, empathy and "deep listening," it is possible to transcend the conflict of interests at the basis of the problem and create a new condition that is equally satisfactory for all parties involved.

Moreover, unlike diplomacy that would foresee the agreements carved in stone, in Galtung's transcend method the agreements are thought of as reversible pacts, from which it is always possible to turn back. This is a condition aimed at favoring the agreement and protecting the contractors. No doubt the underlying hope is that there is no need to resort to this option, and that the operation of transcending the original conflict will continue in a process of transcendence of any further opposition of interests that may arise over time.

## The development theory, the theory of civilization and peace economics

The development theory is proposed through the formulation of fifteen theses that undermine the principles of neo-liberal economics and offer an alternative, and extremely innovative, point of view in contrast to traditional economic arguments. With regard to these arguments Galtung recognizes that the capitalist system not only distorts the relations of exchange and distribution but also the functioning of social institutions that should guide economic behavior. Similarly, Polanyi (1944) recognizes that it is the ideology of the self-regulated market system that favors capital absolutism, but in Polanyi's critique of hypercapitalism he views the financial economy as an unproductive economic activity that colonizes foreign markets, creating imbalances and bubbles in the real market that take the place of productive economic activity.

Three fundamental assumptions of the theory of development must be inserted into this framework: "Development is the unfolding of a culture, the implementation of the code or cosmology of that culture" (Galtung 1996: 127); "development is the progressive satisfaction of the needs of human and non-human nature, starting from those who need it most" (128);[2] and "Development is economic growth but at the expense of no one" (129).

This last assumption is the springboard for discourse on "externalities," that is, on those bipolar variables that reflect positive and negative *inputs* and *outputs* of an economic cycle. They can be ignored by the *mainstream* economy, not counted as a choice of a certain economic practice or not monetized (Galtung 1996: 155). These are therefore side effects normally ignored in the calculations of classical economic theories. That is why there can be no criticism of the aid practices of Western civilization, which perceives itself as universal and for this reason universalizes its developmental experiences and tries to export them to the outside world. In this context, in fact, development is Western development characterized by the logic of capital proper to the capitalist system.

Beyond the skepticism and the criticism of the neo-liberal system and the neo-liberal theory of development, it cannot be denied that

> the economy, the organization of the organization–production–consumption cycle, plays a primary role in a society. On the other hand, the same can be said for the *political ordering*, the organization of power; for *culture*, because culture has a fundamental role in defining what to produce and consume, and how; and for *military ordering*, the organization of coercive power.
>
> (Galtung 1996: 139)

Galtung furthermore distinguishes six economic schools (Galtung 1996: 139–53) and formulates an eclectic development theory taking the best from each.

### Blue school of market and capital

The blue school was based on Smith's theories and followed the capitalist logic characterized by: individualism, verticalism, monetization, processing, expansion and nature. What does this mean? It means that this economic school was based on a precise culture with peculiar characteristics. For example, *individualism* was found not only in the creation of products for individual use but also in the strong competitiveness of the market within which individuals and macro-individual subjects could show their entrepreneurial courage (Galtung 2012: 103). Moreover, individualism allowed the birth of a competitive relationship of the seller struggling for the best sale and the consumer for the best price.

*Verticalization* was above all due to the possession and exclusive control of private property. This means that the owners had control of production factors, working conditions, quantity and quality of products, and marketing by deciding or influencing the taste of buyers. Verticality was also a vehicle for exploitation and iniquity. This could be of four types: unequal exchange between the center (where goods were produced) and the periphery (which provided the raw materials), unequal exchange between those who defined and solved the problems and those who worked according to a "standard operating procedure," unfair exchange in trade, and unequal exchange between generations depriving the later of these of the necessary factors (Galtung 2012: 104).

As for the *monetization*, it was much more than a simple relationship of prices and products. It was the view that anything had a price and that could subsequently be purchased with money. This implied that anything would be marketable and purchasable by the highest bidder.

As for *manufacturing*,

> imprinting culture, C, on nature, N, and increasing C/N, is mirrored inside the firm by employing increasing numbers of increasingly processed humans, meaning R&D specialists. Products have to become increasingly sophisticated, removed from nature. Moreover, the market has to reflect the trend with increasingly complex transactions of increasingly complex products, meaning increasing transaction costs, meaning marginalizing the lesser and more peripheral actors (individuals, firms, countries).
>
> (Galtung 2012: 104)

*Expansion* instead manifested itself in four areas: increase in the quantity and volume of products and transactions, expansion of economic cycles over larger territories, expanding and implementing various economic organizations. It was a continuous and unlimited expansion.

And finally, *nature*, which also included people exposed to tedious, dangerous, dirty and degrading jobs. According to Galtung, in this economic school they were the greatest losers in an incessant economic process that had become an end in itself.

### Red school of state and power

The starting point for the red school was the crisis of the blue school. While the blue school was based on Smithism, the red was based on

Marxism, which is a kind of analysis aimed at revealing the weaknesses of the blue school. However, the two schools were more similar than previously thought, both being based on vast hierarchies, large corporations, and vast bureaucracies. Not to mention the fact that both systems had an elite class of people making decisions about large numbers of others.

Because of these similarities Galtung focused his attention on the denial that the latter moved closer to the former to understand where and how they differed.

Firstly, in the red school the *state* was the *owner*, or at least the controller of the entire production cycle (capital, labor, resources, technology, management, etc.) but also of the distribution channels and mechanisms. An essential aspect was the *planned economy*, namely an economy in which planning, distribution and consumption were centralized and there were no market alternatives. The *priority* of this type of production was the *production of basic goods*, that is to say high productivity of food, clothing, housing and the necessities of health and education. Similar to the role of profit in the blue economy, realizing the plan in the red economy became an end in itself.

Another distinguishing feature was the attitude towards *work*. It too, in the red school, had become an end in itself, as the main objective of the state was to maintain full employment.

Finally, there was the problem of monetization of state-controlled production within the red system. It provided that the factors of production were not for sale. Workers could not choose who to sell their workforce to or even from whom to buy, while managers had fixed wages. This guaranteed that the basic goods were cheap even if scarce. Furthermore, low levels of monetization also served to limit the financial economy.

### *The green school of society and dialogue*

"If the Red school is a weak negation of the Blue, the Green school is a strong negation" (Galtung 2012: 107). The green school was in fact a system based on civil society and on local economic cycles, without national, transnational or international plans. The local economy produced and consumed its own products. The structures that characterized it were small, horizontal, not fragmentary, and continually invested with work integration, rotation and reconstruction. All characteristics that resulted in small economic organizations (with no more than thirty employees) so that everyone was important to each other and hierarchies could not be established (Galtung 2012: 108).

In this economic system the relevant element was not so much economic growth or profit – as in the two previous schools – but respect for and development of nature, respect for people and their development as human beings with emotions, feelings and psyches as well as their corporeality, and the development of societies and the entire world. This is why the main aspects of this school were:

*Production for need, not for greed:* Yet this statement did not answer the question: where does greed start?

*Organization on a human scale*: The idea was to change all organizations (even non-economic ones) to make sure that people felt comfortable within them. However, this did not necessarily mean reducing productivity levels.

*Replacement production:* It was a norm to counteract reckless expansionism.

*Focus on the local market:* The intention was to meet, with limited production, the needs of the local market without having to consider a national or world market.

*The carrying capacity of the planet:* It was a question that had always been asked in the countries of the green school, but that those of the blue and red schools were only now beginning to put to themselves.

### Pink school as a combination of blue, red and even green (every now and then)

The pink school held sway in the social democratic economies of Europe, Canada and the Northern countries. These used a mixed economy (or trading economy) whose main mechanisms were derived from an elitist dialogue between the private and public sectors. A system where elements of capitalism and socialism coexisted, but where some elements of the green system were missing, such as respect for nature, small cooperatives, and references to equality (Galtung 2012: 110). If indeed this rule applied to the larger countries that had recourse to the pink school, in the smaller ones and in those more distant from the big economic arenas, the ideas of the school had managed to better resist the attacks of the green and the red partly because they represented small companies compared with those of the red and blue economies of the United States and the Soviet Union. The pink school therefore located itself in the intersection of the previous three.

### Yellow school as a combination of the blue and red ones

This was the economic school that in the 1990s attracted worldwide attention, and included Japan and China, and the Asian Tigers – South Korea, Taiwan, Hong Kong and Singapore. It differed from the pink by not having within it the elements that characterize the green school and by having succeeded in combining within it two dominant and apparently irreconcilable factors: the market and the state, capital and power. The difficulty in harmoniously combining two systems that should have been in conflict with each other was overcome by the social peculiarity of the Asian region, whose culture allowed this type of contradiction both in theory and in practice, requiring individuals to work hard and with determination.

### *Eclectic school as a combination of the green, pink and yellow ones*

Drawing on a balance of what has been said so far, it can be remarked that the main economic schools, those that were the basis of every system, were blue, red and green. However, all three presented elements of vulnerability related to their fundamental characteristics not being in harmony with the risks of the real world.

The blue school would have risked collapsing if there had been a market crisis and no strong state to lean on. The red one because it had to necessarily enjoy popular support and discipline so as not to risk collapse due to the absence of a real market and a local economy. Green instead was vulnerable because it was easily prey to the speculative interventions of the strongest economies and the flows of migration to the cities (Galtung 2012: 111).

The solutions adopted by the pink and yellow schools had tried to combine the various approaches to ensure that even if one of the three systems collapsed they could still rely on the other two.

But the best economic school could only be the eclectic combination of green, pink and yellow.

> The Eclectic, or "Rainbow," School proposed here goes one step further, pouring much Green into the Pink and Yellow mixes. With three highly diverse components in symbiotic interaction, the economy should become quite resilient. If the most vulnerable systems are Blue and Red, then they should be used indirectly in combinations like Pink and Yellow as building blocks. Never Market, nor State nor Local alone; combine them for resilience and synergy; the famous "more than the sum of the parts." But the Eclectic has no representative.
>
> (Galtung 2012: 112)

## The main critics of Galtung's theory

As one can imagine, such a vast and complex theoretical and methodological system (which we have just made reference to here) would be very much a source of discussion, appreciation and criticism. The most well-known and articulated of these were made by Kenneth Boulding in 1977 in an article titled "Twelve Friendly Quarrels with Johan Galtung." While appreciative of the immense work done by his Norwegian friend, the American economist and sociologist highlighted in twelve points what he considered to be the major weaknesses of Galtung's methodological framework.

For the sake of brevity, we will list them quickly below:

1  Belonging to the category of structuralists, Galtung reasoned mainly through static schemes and static forms. This meant that his thought was intended to analyze existing social structures and was based on the assumpton that they would continue into the future. His thought therefore gave no attention to the evolution of society.
2  His thinking was highly normative, and this represented a risk because "our norms act as a filter which leads to a perversion of our image of reality" (Boulding 1977: 77).
3  His thought was very taxonomic, and this represented a convenience for the human mind rather than a description of reality.
4  Galtung describes society in terms of dichotomies (structural violence vs. behavioral violence, top dogs vs. under dogs), neglecting the random events that occur in social systems.
5  The choice to semantically distinguish positive and negative peace was deceptive. There was no negative peace, at most there was a negative war. Peace is a phase in a system of warring groups (Boulding 1977: 78).
6  Peace is a relative concept.
7  His passion for equality and his hatred for all that is hierarchical make us think that he would welcome "the last ultimate whimper of the universe, according to the second law of thermodynamics, in which all things are at an equal temperature and equally distributed through space so that nothing more can conceivably happen [...]" (Boulding 1977: 79), and fail to recognize that this emphasis on equality has negative effects on another fundamental value: freedom.
8  Galtung totally rejected the idea of hierarchy as the principle of social organization, forgetting that hierarchies are the price to pay for the functioning of organizations that go beyond small groups. Hierarchies are also essential for efficiency in coporate communications.
9  Poverty is not always due to violence. Sometimes it depends on culture, behavior and social dynamics.
10  Poverty depends on production rather than redistribution. History has amply proven that poverty is not fought through distribution, but through the diffusion of *know-how*.
11  Galtung's central–periphery system sometimes obscured the relationship between production, trade and raw materials.
12  Galtung's idea of equality posed limits and criticalities in the perception of the optimal mixture of associative and dissociative elements (which

he tended to divorse) both in relation to conflict resolution and to the improvement of the human condition.

As we can see, Boulding had intended to highlight only the cornerstones of Galtung's thinking, which he said were inconsistent with the evolutionary theory of the social sciences.

Other critics preferred to dwell on some aspects rather than others of Galtung's theories. Consider Godfried van Benthem van den Bergh (1972: 77–85) who intended to highlight the taxonomy of Galtung's imperialist structures in his two-nation model, or Harriet Friedmann and Jack Wayne who explained how, in the discourse of center and periphery, Galtung spoke of imperialism

as that type of bilateral relationship between a central nation and a peripheral one that features a particular harmony of interest (between the two centres) and particular disharmonies of interest (between each centre and its periphery and between the two peripheries). The bilateral relations thus cumulate in a series of hierarchies of nations ("feudal interaction structures"), and there are, apparently, competing empires.

(Friedmann and Wayne 1977: 405)

However, given that he was attempting to treat imperialism and under-development independently of capitalism, this contrast seems to bring us back to a vision of the world divided between great powers.

There are also those who, like Erich Weede and Horst Tiefenbach (1981: 274), have merely noted that the notion of the inegalitarian impact of vertical commerce has not received the necessary methodological support.

## Notes

1  Galtung and Næss 1955.
2  See the concept of *"basic needs."*

## References

Altieri, R. (2008) Johan Galtung e le scienze per la pace. In Galtung, J., *Affrontare il conflitto: trascendere e trasformare*. Pisa: Plus.

Bergh, G. van B. van den (1972) Theory or taxonomy? Some critical notes on Johan Galtung's "A Structural Theory of Imperialism." *Journal of Peace Research* 9(1), 77–85.

Bonora, G. (2011) *Dolci richiami*. Ancona: Arduino Sacco Editore.

Boulding, K. E. (1977) Twelve friendly quarrels with Johan Galtung. *Journal of Peace Research* 14(1), 75–86.

Friedmann, H., and Wayne, J. (1977) Dependency theory: a critique. *Canadian Journal of Sociology* 2, 399–416.

Galtung, J. (1969). Violence, peace and peace research. *Journal of Peace Research* 6(3), 167–191.

Galtung, J. (1971) A structural theory of imperialism. *Journal of Peace Research 8* (2), 81–117.

Galtung, J. (1981) Social cosmology and the concept of peace. *Journal of Peace Research* 18(2), 183–199.

Galtung, J. (1996) *Peace by Peaceful Means: Peace and Conflict, Development and Civilization*. Oslo: International Peace Research Institute; London: Sage.

Galtung, J. (2000) *Johan Uten Land: på fredsveien gjennom verden* [Johan Lackland: on the path of peace through the world]. Oslo: Aschehoug.

Galtung, J. (2012) *Peace Economics: From a Killing to a Living Economy*. Grenzach-Wyhlen: Transcend University Press.

Galtung, J., and Næss, A. (1955) *Gandhi politiske etikk*. Oslo: Tanum.

Polanyi, K. (1944) *The Great Transformation*. New York: Farrar & Rinehart.

Salio, G. (2016) *Giornalismo di pace*. Torino: Gruppo Abele.

Weede, E., and Tiefenbach, H. (1981) Some recent explanations of income inequality: an evaluation and critique. *International Studies Quarterly* 25(2), 255–282.

# 5 The nonviolent strategy of Gene Sharp

## Life and theoretical influences

Let us now consider the contribution of Gene Sharp to the "secularization" of nonviolence and how, through his philosophical analysis of Gandhian thought, he has come to exclude Gandhi from the theory and practice of nonviolent resistance.

I have highlighted the contribution of Gene Sharp because he is recognized as one of the most important contemporary scholars of nonviolent "direct action." We will discuss the diffusion, success and the critiques of his most important texts, among which are *Gandhi Wields the Weapon of Moral Power: Three Case Histories* (1960), "Exploring the Nonviolent Alternatives" (1970), *The Politics of Nonviolent Action* (1973), *Gandhi as a Political Strategist* (1979), *Social Power and Political Freedom* (1980), *From Dictatorship to Democracy: A Conceptual Framework for Liberation* (1993), *There are Realistic Alternatives* (2003), *Self-liberation* (2009). All these texts have inspired movements opposing totalitarian regimes worldwide.

Thanks to *The Politics of Nonviolent Action* Sharp was named the "Machiavelli of nonviolent action" due to the pragmatic approach taken in that book, and the "Clausewitz of nonviolent warfare" (Weber 2004: 232) for his writings on power and the use of nonviolent strategies in struggles for political change.

Born in 1928 in Ohio to a family where the father was a traveling Protestant minister, in 1949 Sharp received a bachelor of arts degree in the social sciences at Ohio State University with a thesis on the war. In the same university, in 1951, with a dissertation titled "Nonviolence: A Sociological Study," he also obtained a master's degree in sociology.

A revised and corrected chapter of his thesis was afterwards published with the title "The Meaning of Nonviolence":

Here Sharp noted that largely thanks to Gandhi, the ideals of nonviolence and methods of nonviolent social action had risen to "sufficient prominence that they must be reckoned with in world thinking and events." He also pointed out that despite this awareness there is much confusion surrounding the term and set out to "clarify, classify and define" various forms of nonviolence in a value-neutral way.

(Weber 2004: 232)

After moving to New York to continue his studies on the history of nonviolence and nonviolent action, he wrote his first book: *Gandhi Wields the Weapon of Moral Power: Three Case Histories.* This was an in-depth analysis of Gandhi's political commitment, which was published only in 1960 in India, but which won the support of Albert Einstein who wrote the preface.

Already in this first period, the peculiarity of Sharp's thought, that it freed nonviolence of the moral and religious aspect that had until then attached to it, began to take shape. In describing Gandhi's political work, in fact, Sharp focused his attention more on the practical and technical than on the moral aspects.

In 1953 he was sentenced to two years in prison for opposing conscription during the Korean War. He obtained his freedom on parole after nine months of detention.

Once he was released from prison he became the personal secretary of Abraham J. Muste, one of the founders of the American pacifist movement. And from 1955 to 1958 he lived in London where he worked as an editorial assistant for the *Peace News*, the most important British magazine on the themes of peace and nonviolence.

From 1958 to 1960 he was a guest of the Institute for Social Research in Oslo, as a Research Fellow, and under the guidance of Arne Næss – who, as we have seen, was also the mentor of Galtung – continued to deepen the thought of Gandhi. During those years Sharp affirmed his credibility as an intellectual so much as to be hosted first as a student, then as a researcher, by American universities of the first level such as the University of Massachusetts, Boston University, the Center for International Affairs of Harvard University, Brandeis University, etc.

In 1968 he obtained a doctorate in philosophy from the Faculty of Social Studies of Oxford University with a thesis in political theory of 1,500 pages entitled "The Politics of Nonviolent Action: A Study in the Control of Political Power." This work would become the basis of the three volumes published between 1973 and 1979 with the title *The Politics of Nonviolent Action* and constitute a very important first piece of Sharp's extensive subsequent research.

## What happened to Gandhi? Discourses on the method of nonviolence

We can ideally distinguish two phases of Sharp's thought: the youthful phase totally oriented to the study of Gandhi's nonviolence and the mature phase characterized by the "secularization" of nonviolence and the choice of a more realistic and pragmatic approach to the objectives of study and action.

As can be seen in the main titles of Gene Sharp's works, above, in the youthful period and up to the 1960s, the philosopher is totally interested in studying the figure of the Mahatma, his action, and the moral justifications of his nonviolence. As Weber notes (2003: 252), Sharp acknowledged Gandhi's effort and success in making nonviolent methods of social action valid, well-defined and incontestable, while admitting a need to "clarify, classify, and define" the term rigorously and scientifically (Sharp 1959: 66).

In particular, Sharp identified nine types of generic nonviolence: non-resistance, active reconciliation, moral resistance, selective nonviolence, passive resistance, peaceful resistance, nonviolent direct action, *satyagraha* and nonviolent revolution (Sharp 1959: 46). None of these types of nonviolence were conceived as a closed container but each left it open that

> there is no strict separation between some of these types, and particular causes may not seem to fit exactly into any of them. This classification should be viewed simply as a tool to facilitate understanding and study of the phenomena, a tool which is neither perfect nor final but may nevertheless be useful.
>
> (Sharp 1959: 46)

Though recognizing the need for further study, Sharp remained strongly attached to Gandhian nonviolence so much so that as he would later write, "we must become integrated loving individuals. Unless people can sense in our lives that of which we speak, it is useless for us to talk of a new way of life" (Sharp 1960: xiii). This is a discourse that made extensive use of philosophical categories and of Gandhi's own language concerning love and the conquest of the adversary from within. The Gene Sharp of this period is an idealistic youth, and so much rooted in the ethics of the Mahatma that he also uses his language, expository methods and rhetoric.

Starting from late 1960s, however, a change began to emerge in the work of our philosopher. In the wake of Sharp's studies at the University of Oxford, in 1970 he published *Gandhi as a Political Strategist* and in one of his essays (dating back to 1962),

Sharp states his position regarding power [...] by noting that "hierarchical systems ultimately depend upon the assistance of the underlings," using a collection of quotations of the Mahatma to make the case. Sharp notes, "Gandhi was probably the first consciously to formulate over a period of years a major system of resistance based upon this assumption."

(Weber 2003: 254)

At that time, we began to see what would later have seemed the natural evolution of Sharp's thought: the "secularization" of nonviolence, the freeing of the concepts and methods of struggle of all the ethico-religious contents that made the comprehension and the application of the techniques of nonviolence a complex issue. Sharp, in fact, in those years noticed that Gandhi's thought was difficult to understand outside of India because the Gandhian message was strongly rooted in the culture, religion and language of that country. Reaffirming Gandhi's thought from the point of view of political strategy meant taking the first step in a qualitative development that would have allowed nonviolence to succeed in America (Sharp 1979: 2) and worldwide.

The most accomplished mature work in this sense is *The Politics of Nonviolent Action* published for the first time in 1973. It was a work that brought together many of Sharp's previous ideas and analyses. Given Sharp's incredible devotion to Ghandhi's accomplishments, it was surprising to discover that the name of Mohandas Karamchand Gandhi did not appear once in the whole text. This clearly meant the complete independence of our author from his illustrious predecessor.

## On nonviolent action policy

Let's now take a closer look at what the *Politics of Nonviolent Action* consisted of. The study was divided into three parts – which in the Italian edition of the Abel Group correspond to three volumes – respectively entitled *Power and Struggle, The Methods of Nonviolent Action* and *The Dynamics of Nonviolent Action*.

The first part included three chapters: the first on the nature and control of political power; the second, on the structural basis of political power; and the third, on nonviolent active struggle.

As can be seen from its structure, the focus of the dissertation was on the nature of political power and the mechanisms that ensured its permanence, reinforcement or end. This was an attempt to identify the strengths and weaknesses of the system so that it would be possible to exploit this knowledge to change it. Afterwards, Sharp developed his concept of power by focusing on the ways and means by which power was strengthened by identifying its real interdependence with the consent of citizens:

> What are the sources of political power? Sharp (1973: 11–12) suggests that "political power appears to emerge from the interaction of all or several of the following sources": (1) authority, (2) human resources, (3) skills and knowledge, (4) intangible factors, (5) material resources, and (6) actions. All of these sources, Sharp points out, depend on the obedience and cooperation of those subject to the power.
>
> (Lipsitz and Kritzer 1975: 725)

If these were the sources of political power, it was now necessary to understand the reasons for the obedience and consent of citizens. In this regard, Sharp identified seven fundamental reasons: habit, fear of sanctions, moral obligation, personal interest, psychological identification with the ruler, indifference or apathy, and the absence of self-esteem (Sharp 1985: vol.1, 64–70). Finally, Sharp introduced the nonviolent method describing it as a particular active form of struggle with its own techniques and strategies.

The second part consisted of five chapters and dealt very precisely with the themes of nonviolent protest and persuasion, the techniques of non-cooperation – also distinguishing between social, economic, and political non-cooperation – and the techniques of nonviolent intervention. This is the most important section of the work since, regardless of one's theoretical frame of reference, because here he made a catalog of 198 (in the beginning, in 1960, there were "only" 63) forms of nonviolent action, also providing explanatory examples.

The third part was dedicated to further discussion of the methods of nonviolent action, its foundations and the importance of having strategies and being prepared for the purpose of applying this technique.

> Nonviolent action is a generic term that includes dozens of specific protest, non-cooperation and non-intervention techniques, in each of which activists carry on the struggle by doing or refusing to do certain things, without resorting to violence. Nonviolent action is therefore not a passive method, *it is not* an absence of action: it is an action that is nonviolent.
>
> (Sharp 1985: vol. 1, 127)

In particular, Sharp tended to underline the importance of the careful preparation of an effective strategy that would weaken the power and consent of the adversary. If this instrument is used successfully, the forces of resistance would benefit not only in terms of freedom, but also in terms of increasing numbers and consensus.

## The Machiavelli of nonviolence

Gene Sharp has been characterized in many ways throughout his career. One of these characterizations was given him by William B. Watson, professor of modern European history of the Massachusetts Institute of Technology, who called him the "Machiavelli of nonviolence" (Soccio 1985: 19).

The professor's intention was not to say that Sharp's philosophical point of view was amoral and based on the viability of coercion and calculation as in the case of Machiavellian political thought, but to underline Sharp's propensity for the study of nonviolence as a science. Just like Machiavelli, who had studied history in order to construct his own theories in a way more objective and free of bias, so too, Sharp has stripped nonviolent thought of values, judgments and morals through a scientific approach to the subject. Just as Machiavelli refrained from evaluating acts through their ends, so Sharp assessed nonviolent political activism by its effectiveness.

Sharp assumed a scientific attitude to the problem before him, that of stripping nonviolence of idealism and ethical values that too often condemned this method to inapplicability, making it a foreign notion, incomprehensible to all those who did not know and affirm the system of principles and values of Hindu culture. He probably understood that the technique stripped of ethico-religious aspects could be applied in any situation and in any context. The objective was therefore to achieve the universal scope of pragmatism, knowledge that could be for everyone, regardless of geographical context, culture, faith, sex or religion. It was about bringing nonviolence out from the isolation of incomprehension to make it a tool for the political struggles of contemporary society.

Bringing nonviolence to the status of a science – as Sharp would have liked to do – meant understanding the history of nonviolence (Soccio 1985: 20), knowing it in all its theories and in all its facets, recognizing its weaknesses and strengths, and finally re-establishing it on new premises. In this sense, Watson saw Sharp as "the Machiavelli of nonviolence."

As noted above, another common feature of Machiavelli and Sharp consisted of the desire to introduce a new kind of measurement to establish the value of political action that did not include either morals or religion. In fact, the value of political activism could only be determined by the choice of the means by which this could be carried forward and by their effectiveness.

Sharp was convinced that nonviolent action could have been used more widely and effectively if people were convinced of its effectiveness by seeing it applied. For this reason, he focused his attention on the practice of nonviolence, neglecting other aspects.

In fact, nonviolent political activism did not require those who applied it to love their enemy, as Gandhi had taught; it had been applied successfully in the past by people who hated their adversaries and wished to impose their own will on them (Soccio 1985: 21). That is why Sharp did not pursue an ideal of perfection, but concrete objectives that depended solely on the good will of those who put them into practice.

## The Von Clausewitz of nonviolent warfare

Since the fundamental problem was essentially that of the effectiveness of nonviolence, Sharp devoted much of his attention to the study of the most incisive actions, or better to the strategy that would best enabled the achievement of the desired results. Just because he considered nonviolence a form of struggle, he decided to learn the lessons of Von Clausewitz in *Vom Kriege* (*"On War"*) and to apply as much as possible of his teachings on military strategy to the strategies of nonviolence.

In an interview by Afif Safieh in the *Journal of Palestine Studies* and dating back to 1987, Sharp explained:

> Clausewitz was not focusing on why war is noble, or even why it is supposedly necessary. Instead, his book, *On War*, is an exercise in the use of one's mind in formulating strategies to oppose the enemy. That is a lesson people of all good causes need to ponder. It is not enough simply to assert goals and objectives. We must think very carefully about how to use the available resources to give us the maximum opportunity to achieve those goals.
>
> (Sharp and Safieh 1987: 38)

Sharp was therefore convinced that it was never enough to act according to morality to obtain results; on the contrary, it was essential to identify the objectives and design tactics and strategies especially suited to achieving them. In this regard, history was able to offer many examples of both winning strategies and failures, and the reasons for these failures.

This intuition represents an extremely important moment in that process of "secularization" of nonviolence towards mere technique – technique that can be learned from the art of war. Certainly, this cannot mean applying the same strategies of violence, but bringing back and adapting that heritage to the context of nonviolence.

There were some principles of military strategy that could not be imported such as surprise, which could have provoked a very violent repression; secret intrigue, incompatible with the need for nonviolent action; or any of the principles and strategies that included the use of brute force, damage and killing.

Sharp was therefore attempting to secure an advantage for nonviolent political action, giving up none of its principles but adding a scientific outlook that could make it more effective.

## From dictatorship to democracy through realistic alternatives

The convictions developed in the early 1970s were repeatedly revised until, in 2002, Gene Sharp published *From Dictatorship to Democracy: A Conceptual Framework for Liberation*.

This was a book written at the request of a Burmese democratic exile, U Tin Maung Win, active in the resistance to the regime of his country of origin through the publication of the *Khit Pyaing* (*Journal of the New Era*). The essay set out to be a real guide to liberation, but since the author did not sufficiently know the social and political situation of the country to which the work was directed, he merely gave general suggestions:

> The essay was originally published in installments in *Khit Pyaing* in Burmese and English in Bangkok, Thailand, in 1993. Afterwards it was issued as a booklet in both languages (1994) and in Burmese again (1996 and 1997). The original editions of the booklet from Bangkok were issued with the assistance of the Committee for the Restoration of Democracy in Burma.
>
> It was circulated both surreptitiously inside Burma and among exiles and sympathizers elsewhere. This analysis was intended only for use by Burmese democrats and various ethnic groups in Burma that wanted independence from the Bruman-dominated central government in Rangoon.
>
> (Sharp 2010: 88)

Although the text had been written and drafted with Burma in mind, the generality of the discussion meant that the work circulated among the resistance groups of various countries and the techniques were also applied in different realities such as the Belgrade of the presidency of Milošević.

The work opened with the declaration that no dictatorship could ever remain standing without three fundamental elements: the subjugation of people, support (both active and passive) and the obedience of citizens to laws, even unjust ones. The organization of mass disobedience could make this balance of elements fragile and, if on account of the likely repression that would have ensued, the dictatorship continued to remain on its feet, it would have been easier to overthrow the now weakened regime.

The discussion continued strongly emphasizing the importance of knowing the conditions of the country where action was take place and identifying the Achilles heel of the regime to be broken down, to have the ability to organize a detailed and accurate strategy.

Let's say that even in the case of *From Dictatorship to Democracy* the strategies and techniques described were no different from those explored in *Politics of Nonviolent Action*, even if the intentions and purposes were of a completely different kind.

As in the *Politics of Nonviolent Action*, our author once again emphasized the difference between the three great categories of nonviolent action: (1) protest and persuasion, (2) social, economic or political non-cooperation, and (3) nonviolent intervention.[1] Moreover, as in his previous encyclopedic work, he recalled the importance of transparency and information both on the objectives that one wanted to achieve and the means to be employed, so as to be able to gain as much approval and support as possible.

Subsequently, Sharp explained that the change could be made to come about through precise mechanisms: first of all, nonviolent struggle would favor social change and a change in context that would have conditioned the opponent's future way of acting. Once the nonviolent action was taken, it was possible to undertake three different tactics: "accommodation," when action proved to ineffectual in the adversary's eyes and the latter was able to calm the situation; "nonviolent coercion," that is, the general refusal to cooperate both in social and economic terms and in politics; and "disintegration," that is, a general challenge on the part of everyone, including bureaucracy, police and armed forces. The aim of bringing down a dictatorship could therefore only be the result of careful and meticulous strategic preparation that should permeate every area of society and the politico-institutional organization of the country. The objective pursued would be difficult to achieve without the evaluation of the precise measures to be undertaken and without having foreseen what the results could be.

The work then continued by explaining step by step how to build follow-up campaigns and how to manage the successes, failures and unexpected results that could confront the organizers.

Finally, Sharp came to express his three conclusions: (1) changing a dictatorship was possible with the means and strategies of nonviolence, (2) to achieve a given objective, careful planning of the strategy was necessary, (3) essential vigilance, hard work and discipline in the struggle were the decisive weapons of all nonviolent resistance.

These conclusions were even more to be expected in view of what was stated in 2003:

it is important to recognize that conflict in society and politics is inevitable and, in many cases, desirable. Some conflicts can be resolved by mild methods, such as negotiation, dialogue, and conciliation – methods that involve compromise.

(Sharp 2003: 1)

When the conflicts were such as not to allow compromise, it was always necessary to bear in mind that an alternative to the use of violence was possible and that this could bring about (if seriously managed) far greater benefits than those obtainable through the use of force.

## Academic critiques of Sharp

Over the years, the works of Sharp have been the subject of appreciation and criticism, mostly in regard to *The Politics of Nonviolent Action* in 1973.

There were those like Carl Friedrich who claimed that Sharp's vision of power was not as original as the author had been led to think, and that he neglected to consider magisterial contributions on the subject such as those of Charles Merriam and Bertrand Russell (Friedrich 1974: 465). The Harvard professor also noted that Sharp's focus on direct violence represented a weakness because it did not consider the psychological violence that had also been employed for example in the Soviet Union (Friedrich 1974: 466).

Lipsitz and Kritzer (1975: 730) on the other hand noted that Sharp, unlike Gandhi, had failed to focus on the difference between nonviolence and violence. Indeed, Sharp seemed to regard nonviolence as the absolute will to not cause suffering to an opponent, while Gandhi's nonviolence was not like this. Nonviolent action in the Gandhian perspective was a type of action in which those who practiced nonviolence tried to avoid inflicting suffering on their opponents. Nonviolent activists preferred to suffer themselves rather than direct suffering to others. Although those who practiced nonviolent action tried to avoid as much as possible causing suffering to their opponents, even if it meant being the cause of suffering to themselves, Gandhi never gave absolute value to this principle, because he was aware of the fact that in every suffering was intrinsic:

While Sharp considers the role of suffering in nonviolent action (1973: 551–555), he does not view the attitude toward suffering as the key distinguishing feature of nonviolence; his primary concern is that with nonviolent action the net suffering will be less than if violent alternatives are chosen. While Sharp sees nonviolent action as clearly distinct from violence (see 1973: 64–67), the interpretation of nonviolence presented above, and the view of nonviolence that can be attributed to Gandhi after the Ahmedabad fast, views the distinction as relative rather than as absolute; the behavior of one group cannot be viewed in isolation from the effect of the behavior on the other group, or in isolation from the behavior of the other group.

(Lipsitz and Kritzer 1975: 730)

In fact, Sharp neglected the importance of suffering in the conduct of nonviolent action. He probably chose not to consider suffering because he abstracted from the ethical aspects of nonviolence to reduce it to pure technique.

Still in connection with this topic quite generally, Thomas Weber pointed out that, as shown by Sharp's work, not all conflicts were or could be solved, indeed, some had to be won. An argument that was in stark contrast to the nonviolence of *satyagrahi* whose goal was to resolve the conflict by transforming the heart of the adversary, and when that had not been possible to contribute equally to transformng the actual conditions of individuals affected by the conflict itself (Weber 2003: 261). In this light nonviolence was not a game of forces, but a process that was going to affect the soul of the individual. A process of changing society by peaceful means.

Also, according to Weber, Sharp had failed to emphasize the positive potentials associated with the use of nonviolence, as he had not been able to focus on the transformative effects (Weber 2003: 262) that he could implement not only at the political but also at the social level. For this reason, Sharp's nonviolence could be considered merely a technique, an instrument to achieve set objectives.

Beyond the criticism, however, no one doubts the value of Sharp's work. In a situation of physical, academic and political isolation, he managed to systematize and classify meticulously the techniques of nonviolence, objectifying and stripping it of all those elements that made it difficult to understand outside the Indian context.

Academic isolation has not been matched by lack of influence, however. On the contrary, the success of the incessant work of Sharp came precisely from nonviolent activist groups, including Otpor! in Serbia, Kmara in Georgia, Pora in Ukraine, KelKel in Kyrgyzstan, Zubr in Belarus, not to forget the National League for the Democracy in Burma and the Egyptian activists of the colored revolution. Although few people in the United States know this figure today, in countries recently afflicted with violence or the scene of popular unrest, Sharp is a point of reference, and his *From Dictatorship to Democracy* is one of the most widely read books.

# Note

1  Nonviolent intervention corresponds to psychological, physical, social, economic or political means, such as fasting, nonviolent occupation, and parallel government (forty-one methods) used in the framework of nonviolent struggle. Civil disobedience is a subcategory of political intervention, which is in turn a subcategory of the more general nonviolent intervention.

# References

Friedrich, C. (1974) Review of *The Politics of Nonviolent Action*, by Gene Sharp. *Political Theory* 2(4), 465–467.

Lipsitz, L., and Kritzer, H. M. (1975) Unconventional approaches to conflict resolution: Erikson and Sharp on nonviolence. *Journal of Conflict Resolution* 19(4), 713–733.

Sharp, G. (1959) Meanings of non-violence: a typology (revised). *Journal of Conflict Resolution* 3(1), 41–66.

Sharp, G. (1960) *Gandhi Wields the Weapon of Moral Power: Three Case Histories*. Ahmedabad: Navajivan.

Sharp, G. (1973) *The Politics of Nonviolent Action*. Boston: Porter Sargent.

Sharp, G. (1979) *Gandhi as a Political Strategist*. Boston: Porter Sargent.

Sharp, G. (1985) *Politica dell'azione nonviolenta*, vol. 1: *Potere e lotta*; vol. 2: *Le tecniche*; vol. 3: *La dinamica*. Torino: Edizioni Gruppo Abele, <https://www. aeinstein.org/wp-content/uploads/2013/11/The-Politics-of-Nonviolent-Action-Vo lume-I-Italiansmallpdf.com_.pdf>,<https://www.aeinstein.org/wp-content/uploa ds/2014/01/The-Politics-of-Nonviolent-Action-Volume-II-Italian.pdf>, <https:// www.aeinstein.org/wp-content/uploads/2013/11/The-Politics-of-Nonvio lent-Action-Volume-III-Italiansmallpdf.com_.pdf> (accessed 5 September 2017).

Sharp, G. (2003) *There Are Realistic Alternatives*. Boston: Albert Einstein Institution, <https://www.aeinstein.org/wp-content/uploads/2013/09/TARA.pdf> (accessed 20 September 2017).

Sharp, G. (2010) *From Dictatorship to Democracy*. Boston: Albert Einstein Institution, <https://www.aeinstein.org/wp-content/uploads/2013/09/FDTD.pdf> (accessed 13 September 2017).

Sharp, G., and Safieh, A. (1987) Gene Sharp: nonviolent struggle. *Journal of Palestine Studies* 17(1), 37–55.

Soccio, M. (1985) Introduzione. In Sharp, G., *Politica dell'azione nonviolenta 1: Potere e lotta*. Torino: Edizioni Gruppo Abele, <https://www.aeinstein.org/wp -content/uploads/2013/11/The-Politics-of-Nonviolent-Action-Volume-I-Italia nsmallpdf.com_.pdf> (accessed 5 September 2017).

Weber, T. (2003) Nonviolence is who? Gene Sharp and Gandhi. *Peace & Change* 28(2), 250–270.

Weber, T. (2004) *Gandhi as a Disciple and Mentor*. Cambridge: Cambridge University Press.

# Conclusions

As we have seen from this brief and certainly not exhaustive essay, the contemporary paths of peace and nonviolence have been constantly the objects of mutual influence and sometimes even overlaps that have led the concepts of "peace" and "nonviolence" to be often grossly confused, associated with one another or to be erroneously used interchangeably.

However, as emerges from this study, "nonviolence" and "peace" are two extremely different concepts. Going back to the various uses of these concepts starting from Henry David Thoreau, going through to Mohandas Gandhi, Abdul Ghaffar Khan, Simone Weil, Aldo Capitini, Norberto Bobbio, Danilo Dolci, Johan Galtung and Gene Sharp, we clearly realize that in all the authors considered nonviolence is a method of political protest based on non-cooperation, peaceful intervention in favor of the victims of violence, and public and strategic acts of resistance to the politics of the dominant group (Gallo-Cruz 2011). On peace, on the other hand, the discourse is characterized by a more marked heterogeneity, probably due to the wider extension of the subject in question.

However, by way of conclusion, it is useful to point out that what distinguishes what we might call the "first" authors from the "last" is the ethico-religious aspect.

Although Gandhi and Khan were reformers for action and social change, there is no doubt that they regarded nonviolence as a way of living life, of building peaceful relations, and as an instrument for transforming an adversary's soul through their own suffering. Gandhi and Khan's nonviolence was therefore inextricably bound up with the ethico-religious aspects of their cultural group of belonging.

Moving then to European pacifism, with Simone Weil, this strong interconnection between religious morality and nonviolence suffered the first jolts. Despite the fact that she was a mystic, Weil's nonviolence began to deviate from religion as an institution and in particular from the Catholic Church, using the revolutionary arguments of the Marxist matrix linked to the oppression of workers, in the youth phase, and the critique of totalitarianism as religious worship of social reality, in the mature phase. Proof of this deviation is the choice to "stand on the threshold," to never be baptized, to remain among the excluded, the oppressed, the unfortunate.

Aldo Capitini, like Weil, was disillusioned by the Catholic Church, and although intently religious he also decided to deviate from the institution of the Catholic Church in favor of a more intuitive reading of nonviolence and of the relationship with God. He was the first in Europe to turn Gandhian thought into a real politico-social project, giving way to that passage from the purely theoretico-ideal thought linked to nonviolence to concrete projects of social reform, undertaken through COS (Centri di Orientamento Sociale, or Social Orientation Centers) and the Centers for Religious Orientation (Centri di Orientamento Religioso).

In a world plagued by nuclear threat, by brinkmanship and by a fragile balance of power, Norberto Bobbio's contribution to the theme of peace and nonviolence has made a decisive step towards a resolution of the problem. Institutional pacifism aimed precisely at this resolution, identifying principles that could represent the pillars of a supra-state system that would make conflicts impractical, too expensive or counterproductive. It was a secular pacifism that shrugged off moral discourse to take the objective attitude of a science of law.

Danilo Dolci – who was influenced by Capitini and considered him a teacher, a source of inspiration – also went beyond traditional nonviolence, relegating the ideal dimension of his thought to a secondary level, compared with his activism in support of social reform in the local context of the Palermo hinterland. It is certainly true that Dolci was a great scholar and that his political actions were the result of profound studies, and yet his thinking is not made up of ideal societies, ideal institutions or august references to morals. His thought is directed to social redemption in the here and now. Moreover, unlike Weil, his being on the side of the fogotten, the oppressed, his participation in their lives, was not limited to trying out their suffering on himself but became a way to identify and give voice to their skills, to build with them a new society, less violent, more peaceful and more inclusive.

The contribution of Johan Galtung is different. Friend and collaborator of Dolci, he was deeply inspired by the Italian sociologist, from whom he learned the rejection of violence, the distinction between types of peace, the concept of structural violence (although Dolci had never called it that), just to cite a few examples. Galtung is a brilliant, wise thinker who has contributed to the academic framework of peace research, to its ennoblement as a topic of study and research, and to the development of new lines of inquiry. His approach was clearly sociological, and his contributions ranged from research methodology to theories of peace, of conflict, of development and civilization. More than an ideal project of society, Galtung's has been a careful analysis of reality and an incessant work of reform whose purpose was not to achieve an ideal form of government/society, but the fulfillment of basic human needs, the elimination or at least the mitigation of all forms of violence and the exaltation of human potential that allows for individual flourishing.

If Galtung fundamentally focused on the sociological study of peace from a medico-scientific point of view, Gene Sharp was interested in a pragmatic study of the techniques of nonviolence. Although he is commonly considered a philosopher, it is undoubted that his theories of nonviolence rested on a study and a deep sociological knowledge of the dynamics of groups, the factors of inclusion, exclusion, and the concepts of status, power and role.

Moreover, returning for a moment to the *fil rouge* that reoccurs in our text, and which concerns the transformations and the various uses of the concepts of peace and nonviolence, it is undoubted that Sharp has contributed to a radical change in the concept of nonviolence. By stripping it of all ethico-religious or spiritual attributes, he made nonviolence a strategically constructed fighting technique and a tool for politico-social reform. In Sharp there is no ideal, no utopian society, no question of values to promote, but relations of power, tensions, frictions and social contradictions, and techniques to "govern" society. His interest is in demonstrating the efficacy of nonviolence, in elevating it to a scientific method based on abstract and replicable principles, and the results of a systematic study of the narratives of the political struggles of peoples and groups.

It is therefore evident that with progress in history, change in society, and refinement in research techniques, the most intelligible aspects of the thought of the first authors taken into consideration in this study have been abandoned in favor of scientific rigor, of the objectivity of the sciences, of methods with universal scope.

## References

Gallo-Cruz, S. (2011) Global nonviolence. In Ritzer, G., ed., *The Encyclopedia of Globalization*. Oxford: Wiley Blackwell.

# Index

116    *Index*

For Product Safety Concerns and Information please contact our EU
representative GPSR@taylorandfrancis.com
Taylor & Francis Verlag GmbH, Kaufingerstraße 24, 80331 München, Germany

www.ingramcontent.com/pod-product-compliance
Ingram Content Group UK Ltd.
Pitfield, Milton Keynes, MK11 3LW, UK
UKHW021446080625
459435UK00012B/389